Stress Prevention in the Workplace:

Assessing the Costs and Benefits to Organisations

EF/96/09/EN

European Foundation
for the Improvement of
Living and Working Conditions

Stress Prevention in the Workplace:

Assessing the Costs and Benefits to Organisations

by
Professor Cary L Cooper,
Manchester School of Management, University of Manchester,
Institute of Science & Technology, UK

Professor Paula Liukkonen,
Department of Economics,
University of Stockholm, Sweden

Dr Susan Cartwright,
Manchester School of Management,
University of Manchester, Institute of Science & Technology, UK

Loughlinstown, Dublin 18, Ireland
Tel.: (+353) 1 282 6888   Fax: (+353) 1 282 6456

Cataloguing data can be found at the end of this publication

Luxembourg: Office for Official Publications of the European Communities, 1996

ISBN 92-827-6503-2

Printed in Ireland

CONTENTS

Page No.

Chapter 1   The Problem of Workplace Stress   1

Chapter 2   The Case Studies   11

Case Study I - Introduction and Key Points   12

From Taylorism to 1000 objective-oriented groups-
Experiences of a Cultural Revolution in
an Industrial Concern   13

Case Study II - Introduction and Key Points   25

Stress-Related Interventions in Construction Work   26

Case Study III - Introduction and Key Points   48

Stress Management within the Pharmaceutical Industry   49

Chapter 3   The Organizational and Economic Costs of Stress:
A Measurement Perspective   71

Chapter 4   Organizational Stress Intervention Strategies:
Current Practices   85

Chapter 5   Towards the Creation of Healthy Organization -
The Wider Implications   95

References

Useful Names and Addresses

STRESS PREVENTION IN THE WORKPLACE: ASSESSING THE COSTS AND BENEFITS TO ORGANIZATIONS

EXECUTIVE SUMMARY

1. This report has arisen in response to a growing interest and concern amongst researchers, organizations and policymakers throughout the European Union to more positively address the factors responsible for illhealth in the workplace.

2. In the rapidly changing internal and external business environments in which organizations are operating, the pace and attendant pressures continue to place ever-increasing demands on the individual. While the workplace can be challenging and stimulating and enhance well being and happiness, it can also be stressful.

3. Research has shown that mismanaged pressure or excessive stress can adversely affect individual performance, physical health and psychological well being. This has cost implications for the individual, the organization and society more generally. Clearly, there is a need for organizations to understand and count the costs of stress at work and to take action to minimise the health risks to their employees, wherever possible.

4. This report details three European case studies which illustrate how organizations have identified the costs of stress; the kinds of interventions they have subsequently introduced and the ways in which they have demonstrated the cost benefits associated with these interventions.

5. The case studies presented are drawn from the recent experiences of three organizations in Sweden, the Netherlands and the UK. They represent three different industries/business sectors namely electrical manufacturing, construction and pharmaceuticals.

6. The case studies illustrate three different approaches to stress prevention targeted at different levels of employees. Briefly, these approaches involved:-

    - changing aspects of the job and the working environment of industrial production workers in Sweden, through job enlargement and enrichment and the creation of autonomous work teams

    - improving the communication and consultative structure in a Dutch company and providing individual skills training for managers

    - an organizational-wide stress management programme amongst managerial/white collar workers in the UK directed at improving individuals skills and resources and creating a more aware and supportive organizational environment

7. Evidence is presented which seeks to demonstrate how such interventions can produce both qualitative and quantitative benefits. For example, quantitative benefits are considered in terms of the effect of interventions on production costs and absenteeism rates. Qualitative benefits are considered in terms of the positive effect on organization's capacity or competitiveness through the increased flexibility, motivation and enjoyment of work of its workforce.

8. However, in seeking to evaluate the costs and benefits of stress prevention at company level, the case studies also highlight the methodological difficulties in establishing conclusive evaluative evidence. Therefore, the report discusses what lessons can be learnt from the case studies and provides and evaluates methodologies which an organization can practically apply to assess the potential costs and benefits.

9. It also compares and contrasts the approaches to stress prevention exemplified in the case studies within the wider context of the stress research literature and experiences in the field of stress prevention.

10. The report provides information on current practices in the area of stress intervention. In broad terms, there are three types of stress prevention strategies termed primary, secondary and tertiary levels of prevention which address different stages in the stress process.

11. **Primary Prevention** is concerned with taking action to reduce or eliminate stressors (i.e. sources of stress)
    Secondary Prevention is concerned with increasing stress awareness and providing employees with the skills necessary to manage experienced stress more effectively
    Tertiary Prevention is concerned with the rehabilitation and recovery process of those individuals who have suffered or are suffering from serious ill health as a result of stress, usually by the provision of counselling services.

12. Stress prevention would seem to present a means whereby an organization cannot only reduce or contain the costs of employee ill health but can also positively maintain and improve organizational health and productivity. This report may be a useful first step towards the future development of a practical methodology for organizations to enable them to do so.

13. Finally, as occupational stress is not just an organizational problem but a wider societal problem which is ultimately shared by all members of the EU, it considers ways in which EU policymakers could encourage and inform stress prevention activities. These might include economic incentives, specific assistance for small and medium sized enterprises and more information and research.

Chapter 1
The Problem of Workplace Stress

Introduction

Interest in the concept of "healthy organizations", in its wider sense, is gaining prominence amongst researchers, employers and policymakers throughout the European Union (Cooper & Williams, 1994; European Foundation for the Improvement of Living and Working Conditions, 1994).. This has manifested itself in increasing concern to more positively address the factors responsible for ill health in the workplace.

Organizational health extends beyond a simple analysis of the profit and loss account. Profitability is a clear indicator of the success and financial health of an organization at a specific, and hence, in accounting terms, historical point in time. However, it is not necessarily a good predictor of future performance, unless account is taken of the ability of the organization and its workforce to sustain and possibly increase that level of performance over time. An automobile may be running perfectly well one day, despite a neglectful owner, but it is invariably only a matter of time before a costly accident or breakdown occurs. Similarly, the performance and financial health of an organization is dependent upon the physical, psychological and mental health of its members.

There are a range of indices which are indicative of organizational ill health, other than the more obvious data such as sickness absence, high labour turnover and low productivity. These include poor accident and safety records, increased recruitment and related training costs, low levels of organizational commitment and job satisfaction and generally deteriorating industrial and customer relations. In some countries, employee ill health is also reflected in high insurance and healthcare costs.

Against a background of mounting research evidence (Cooper & Cartwright 1994; Cooper & Payne 1988), there can be little dispute that stress has an adverse impact on both individual and organizational health. Links have been consistently demonstrated between excessive stress and a variety of negative outcomes which directly or indirectly affect employee health and well being in the workplace (McLean 1980; Frese 1985; Cooper, 1995). For example, stress has been implicated in the incidence and development of:-

- Coronary heart disease
- Mental illness
- Certain types of cancer
- Poor health behaviours such as smoking, dietary problems, lack of exercise, excessive alcohol consumption and drug abuse
- Life and job dissatisfaction
- Accidents and careless or unsafe behaviours at work
- Marital and family problems
- A whole range of more minor physical and psychological conditions including migraine, stomach ulcers, hay fever, skin rashes, impotence and menstrual problems, insomnia, panic attacks, irritability, poor concentration, anxiety and indecisiveness

In short, stress can make people ill, impairs their day-to-day functioning and relationships with others and reduces their effectiveness in the workplace. In the UK alone, lifestyle and stress related illness accounts for at least half of all premature deaths (Palmer, 1989).

The Financial Costs of Stress

Interest in employee health and the importance of stress prevention has a long history in Europe, especially within the Nordic countries. Traditionally, this interest has been oriented towards implementing changes in the methods and style of work organization and improving the working environment to reduce job strain (Baker 1985; Johnson & Johanson 1991). In many respects, the notion that stress carries monetary costs has tended to be implicit rather than explicit in this approach.

Although occupational stress prevention may have had a shorter history in the USA, it is perhaps fair to say that the more powerful and widely promoted financial arguments as to the potential benefits of stress prevention have emanated from that country. For example, it has been widely documented that US industry loses approximately 550 million working days per year due to absenteeism (Harris et al, 1985). It is estimated (Elkin & Rosch, 1990) that 54% of these absences are in some way stress related. Furthermore, stress is considered to be responsible for between 60%-80% of all workplace accidents. Collectively, the cost of stress to American organizations, assessed by absenteeism, reduced productivity, compensation claims, health insurance and direct medical expenses is in the region of $150 billion per year (approximately ECU 111 billion) (Karasek & Theorell, 1990). Awareness of these costs, combined with stress litigation fears, have provided strong financial incentives for organizations to act to reduce stress and promote employee health in the workplace.

Because US employers are directly responsible for employee healthcare costs, it is relatively easier to quantify these costs than in European economies, where a substantially greater burden is still met through State funded welfare and health services and other agencies. The financial costs may be more dispersed and more difficult to measure and quantify within the European Union, but nevertheless, they exist.

Some indication of the costs of stress can be gained from several recent European and national studies. According to a report (CEC, 1992) on occupational accidents and disease within the EU:-

- Approximately 8,000 people die each year as a result of occupational accidents and disease
- A further 10 million suffer some form of work related accident or disease
- The annual compensation paid for these injuries and illnesses is estimated at ECU 20,000 million

Recent evidence from the UK, and particularly Scandinavia, where the issue of employee welfare has traditionally assumed greater importance than in the rest of Europe, further highlights the growing problem. Figures released by the Confederation of British Industry (Sigman, 1992) calculate that in the UK, 360 million working days are lost annually through sickness, at a cost to organizations of £8 billion (approximately ECU 9.5 billion). Again, it has been estimated by the UK Health & Safety Executive that at least half of these lost days are related to workplace stress. In terms of heart disease alone (Cartwright & Cooper, 1994), the British Heart Foundation suggest heart and circulatory disease accounts for 21% of all male absence; 45% of all premature deaths amongst the working population between 35 and 64 each year; at a cost in lost productive value to the average UK organization of 10,000 employees of £2.5 million (ECU 2.9 million). Overall, the cost of occupational stress in the UK is estimated to amount to over 10% of Gross National Product

(GNP).

A report by the Nordic Council of Ministers (Lunde-Jensen, 1994) calculated the economic costs c
work related sickness and accidents in Denmark, Sweden, Norway and Finland, during the perio
1990-1992. The costs were lowest in Denmark, amounting to over ECU 1,000 for every person i
employment or 2.5% of Denmark's GNP and highest in Norway, amounting to ECU 3,300 pe
employee or 10.1% of GNP (Table 1 below).

Table 1.1 : Cost of Work Related Sickness and Accidents in the Nordic Countries

	Denmark 1990	Sweden 1990	Norway 1990	Finland 1990
Labour force	2.67 million	4.51 million	2.02 million	2.17 million
Total costs per employee	ECU 1000	ECU 1660	ECU 3300	ECU 1500
Total costs as % of GNP 1990 (1992)	2.5%	5.1%	10.1%	3.6%
Occupational accidents	ECU 370 million	ECU 780 million	ECU 370 million	ECU 460 million
Work related sicknesses	ECU 2330 million	ECU 6700 million	ECU 6300 million	ECU 2800 million

Source: Lunde-Jensen, P. (1994). Janus No. 18 (4).

Furthermore, the potential costs of occupational stress are not just confined to the directly
measurable costs which have been outlined above. According to Cooper (1995), organizations
are additionally facing the problem of "presenteeism" i.e. people turning up for work who are
so distressed by their jobs or some aspect of the organizational culture or climate that they
contribute little, if anything, to their work.

Workplace Stress: A Problem for Today and the Future

Occupational stress is likely to be a continuing problem throughout the 90s and beyond. People play a crucial role in the creation of organizational wealth, particularly in the developed western economies, which have become increasingly dependent upon the growth and strength of their service industries. Staff have the biggest impact on costs, typically accounting for between 50%-80% of organizational expenditure; and an even bigger one on revenue. In 1991, the European Commission (1992) conducted a survey on workplace safety and health, of almost 13,000 European workers. The survey found that 48% of respondents considered that their professional work activity affected or could affect their health; of which 42% referred to stress.

Although most people would accept that stress is a widespread feature of modern life, the term has become so much a part of our everyday vocabulary that it often used in a casual and imprecise manner. Consistent with other emotionally charged topics, like sin (Ivancevich & Matteson 1980), it has come to mean different things to different people. Because stress and its effects on people have been studied from the perspectives of a wide range of disciplines (e.g. medicine, health psychology, work psychology) the concept has been variously defined within the general stress literature (e.g. Beehr 1995; Cox 1978; Lazarus 1976; Selye 1946). According to Cummings & Cooper (1979):- "A stress is any force that puts a psychological or physical factor beyond its range of stability, producing a strain within the individual. Knowledge that a stress is likely to occur constitutes a threat to the individual. A threat can cause a strain because of what it signifies to the person".

Whenever a person is subjected to stress a series of hormonal reactions take place, initiated by adrenaline, which are designed to protect the body causing it to prepare for physical action. This is known as the 'Fight or Flight' response. The heart rate increases in order to pump more oxygen around the body, muscle tension increases and blood sugar is released to fuel the exercising muscles. Stress is clearly part of the human condition and everybody needs a certain amount of stress to remain healthy and alert. A few nerves before an important meeting or presentation can be positively beneficial. This kind of positive stress or pressure is stimulating, it gives us a 'buzz' and enhances performance. However, when this pressure or stress becomes long term or excessive to the extent that the individual perceives his/herself unable to cope successfully with a situation and experiences a loss of control the effects of stress become negative and health and performance deteriorate. We all have our own personal 'pressure curves' and stress threshold, at which point pressure becomes too much and develops into negative stress. This threshold will vary between individuals and across different situations.

Long term excessive stress is harmful and escalates the process of 'wear and tear' on the body and leads to the kinds of health problems already mentioned. Researchers investigating stress in the workplace have been concerned with identifying the causes and outcomes of negative stress. A definition provided by Newman and Beehr (1979) summarises the transactional nature of the stress process in the workplace:

> "Job stress refers to a situation wherein job-related factors interact with a worker to change (i.e. disrupt or enhance) his or her psychological and or physiological conditions such that the person (i.e. mind or body) is forced to deviate from normal functioning"

There are several factors which have increasingly become characteristic of the modern day work environment which have contributed to the rising incidence of stress at work.

In recent years, there have been significant changes in the *demographic composition of the workforce; the ownership and structure of organizations and the nature of work itself.*

(i)   A Changing Workforce

Detailed surveys of social and economic trends in the EU show that Europe's population is falling and getting older. Job losses and long term unemployment have tended to have the greatest impact on males over 50. The gender composition of the workforce has also changed dramatically in recent years. In 1993, 39% of the EU workforce was female, with rates varying between 31% (Spain) and 45% (Denmark and the UK) (Davidson & Cooper 1993; Cartwright 1995). Whilst female workers still tend to be concentrated in certain business sectors, e.g. retailing, nursing, education and part-time jobs, the "feminisation" of the workplace has major social and structural implications on work organization.

(ii)   **The Changing Nature of Organizations**

The build up and aftermath of the recession, the growing influence of European legislation in corporate business and the demands of an increasingly global market has changed the shape and structure of many European organizations. Since the 1980's, European organizations have experienced an unprecedented wave of domestic and cross border mergers, acquisitions and strategic alliances. Many more have been involved in major organizational restructuring as a result of privatisation and/or in response to increasing market competition. As traditional organizational structures have become "flatter and leaner", this has had the effect of increasing the workload and demands on the individual.

Inevitably, such radical, rather than incremental, changes have created considerable employee uncertainty and required substantial adaptation and adjustment to changed working practices, managerial style and work culture. Concern regarding job security has become a major feature of the workforce today, particularly in light of the growing trend towards short term working contracts.

(iii)   **The Changing Nature of Work Itself**

Job skills and work demands have also changed significantly. The demands for a more flexible workforce have placed an emphasis on multi-skilling and increasingly suggest that individuals in the future will be expected to pursue multiple careers if they are to remain in employment until the traditional retirement age.

The growth of automation in the workplace, particularly computer technology has steadily increased and revolutionised the traditional office. Technological change involves much more than a change in the method of doing a job; it also represents a major social transformation in the workplace. For some workers, an estimated one quarter to a half of all knowledge based workers in the UK, by the year 2000, it may even mean that the home becomes the workplace.

The potential sources of occupational stress are many and various. However, stress at work is primarily caused by the fundamentals of change, lack of control and a high workload. The evidence would suggest that all of these are characteristic of most organizations today and will continue to remain so in the immediate future.

Corporate Responses to Stress at Work

This type of action taken by organizations has taken many forms. De Frank & Cooper (1987) suggest that stress intervention in the workplace can focus on the individual, the organization or the individual/organizational interface. Interventions which focus on the individual are concerned with extending the physical and psychological resources of employees to enable them to deal more effectively with experienced stress or help them modify their appraisal of a stressful situation and so reduce the threat it presents. Health and stress education, skills training in the area of time management, relaxation techniques or assertive behaviour are examples of such interventions.

In contrast, 'organizationally focused' interventions are concerned with reducing workplace stress by addressing factors which operate at the macro (organizational) level. Such interventions might include changing aspects of the organizational structure, reviewing selection and training procedures, or developing more flexible and 'family friendly' systems and personnel policies which more closely meet the needs and demands of the workforce.

Finally, there are interventions which operate on a more local, work group level, which focus on the individual/organizational interface. These are likely to address issues relating to work relationships and roles, task redesign, employee participation and autonomy.

While there are examples of all three types of intervention within the Europe, by far the most popular form of organizational intervention has tended to be directed at changing the individual and improving their lifestyle and/or stress management skills. Typically, such interventions may involve:-

- the provision of on-site fitness and relaxation/exercise classes
- corporate membership or concessionary rates at local health and fitness clubs
- smoking cessation programmes
- the introduction of cardiovascular fitness programmes
- advice on alcohol and dietary control (particularly cutting down on cholesterol,

salt and sugar)

- the design of "healthy" canteen menus
- regular health checks and health screening
- stress education and advice of lifestyle management more generally
- psychological counselling

Often, organizations offer some combination of these packaged as a multi-modular programme available to employees and possibly their partners.

In recent years, there has been a rapid expansion in individually-oriented stress prevention interventions such as EAPs and health and lifestyle management programmes within the UK and amongst European organizations of US parentage (e.g. Johnson & Johnson). This approach has developed alongside the traditional research and policy efforts characteristic of Sweden and the Netherlands to counter stress at work by focusing on the actual organization of work (de Gier et al., 1994). Although, still relatively few employers within Europe provide programmes as comprehensive or extensive as the US Control Data Corporation's "STAYWELL" or the New York Telephone Company's "WELLNESS" programmes.

Expansion in the area of stress prevention has been rather slower to develop momentum in Europe, perhaps because the financial incentives for doing so are not readily appreciated. The European evidence (Wynne & Clarkin, 1992) suggests that health promotion activities within the EU are more likely to be prompted by Health and Safety legislation and a felt need to improve employee relations and morale rather than reduce absenteeism. It is still the case that most activities focus on safety and interventions to the physical environment. Therefore they are not directly promoted by health but compliance to legislation and regulations. In this respect, the large differences in legislative background relating to workplace health across the member states have contributed to determine activity levels. Furthermore, workplace interventions tend to be confined to large organizations employing more than 500 employees, rather than small and medium sized enterprises in which the majority of working populations in many countries work.

The Aims of this Publication

The continuing problem of stress at work means that organizations will increasingly need to consider the issue of stress interventions. To be effective, stress intervention strategies have to be carefully chosen, integrated and well designed to suit the needs of the organization and its members. Furthermore, they need to be evaluated against specified outcome measures in terms of their effectiveness and costs.

Therefore the aims of this publication are:-

(i) to present case studies from organizations within the EU as examples of current practice in the area of stress management. They serve to illustrate how organizations identify the costs of stress and demonstrate the cost benefits associated with effective stress prevention and management interventions at the workplace; in relation to health, well being, productivity and quality

(ii) to provide and evaluate methodologies to assess these costs and benefits

(iii) to provide information on current practices in the area of stress intervention.

Chapter 2

The Case Studies

Introduction

The Case Studies presented are drawn from the recent experiences of three organizations in Sweden, the Netherlands and the UK. They represent three different industries/business sectors namely electrical manufacturing, construction and pharmaceuticals.

The interventions adopted by these organizations differ in terms of their content and focus. The Swedish case (Case Study I) reports on an organizationally focused intervention to reduce stress by changing aspects of the job and working environment. The intervention is focused at improving the quality of work life of manual workers by increasing employee autonomy and participation and improving job content.

In contrast, the intervention described in the Dutch case (Case Study II) combines elements of both an organizational and individual focused intervention. It addresses stress reduction, through macro level improvements in the communication and consultative structure and also individual skills training. The primary focus of the reported intervention is at managerial level. Although the resultant benefits of the intervention extended to other organizational levels.

Finally, the UK case (Case Study III) reports on an established and wide scale stress management programme, predominantly directed at managerial/white collar workers. Whilst part of a wider strategy, it differs from the other two interventions in that it does not directly attempt to modify the potential sources of stress inherent in the work environment. Instead, it is directed at improving and extending the skills and resources of its individual members and creating a more aware and supportive organizational environment.

In all three cases, encouraging evidence is presented as to the positive outcomes and benefits associated with the interventions.

Case Study I

Asea Brown Boveri AB (ABB)

This case study reports on an intervention strategy designed to change the style of work organization in a Swedish electrical manufacturing company. This was achieved through job enlargement and enrichment, and the creation of autonomous work teams. The intervention was originally introduced in a small department employing approximately 50 workers. Post intervention measures indicate substantial productivity gains and reduction in sickness absence and replacement costs. The success of the intervention is reflected in ABB's decision to extend the initiative throughout the Group.

The main points illustrated by the case study are:-

• the establishment of a range of 'hard' baseline economic indices relating to productivity and employee costs (e.g. sickness/absence, labour turnover) from the outset, by which to evaluate the effects of the intervention.

• the need to establish strong commitment and financial support from Senior Management and other interested parties, e.g. Trade Unions

• the intervention resulted in a 12% reduction in production costs amounting to an annual saving of 1.5 million Swedish Krone (ECU 157,500 approximately), which met the investment costs of the programme in one year

• the benefits of the programme appear to have been replicated in other parts of the organization in that throughput time has reduced by 47% over a three year period

• the organization has benefitted in many other ways which are more difficult to quantify in economic terms but nevertheless important. For example, the organization now has a more flexible workforce. In addition, almost all of its products are currently delivered to the customer within the agreed time.

From Taylorism to 1000 objective-oriented groups
Experiences of a Cultural Revolution in an Industrial Concern
Dr Sven Kvarnstrom, Former Medical Director, ABB Group

Over the past five years in many companies in Sweden there has been a marked trend towards broader job content, increased skills development, greater flexibility, more delegation of responsibility and, not least of all, a marked growth of work in objective-oriented groups with a high degree of autonomous responsibility. This has happened mainly in manufacturing firms, but the tendency to favour this new type of work organization has spread increasingly to the white collar sector.

Many companies have been very successful in their innovation schemes. The company with the greatest mass of accumulated experience of modified work organization in Swedish industry is ASEA Brown Boveri AB, referred to hereafter as ABB. In efforts to inspire companies around the country to new forms of working, the example of ABB is often presented and the innovation process which took place there has been termed a cultural revolution. Other smaller Swedish companies may have been more successful, but ABB's innovation process encompasses the greatest number of useful lessons, especially viewed from a long term perspective.

The ABB Group

ABB is a worldwide undertaking with companies in all part of the globe, and employs a total of about 220,000 staff. In Sweden, ABB has about 29,000 employees in over 100 independent firms. Its main base in Sweden is Västeras, where about 10,000 people are employed, and it is in this location that the observations forming the basis of this case study were collected.

Diversified manufacture in the electrical equipment sector

Electrical equipment of different types is manufactured by ABB's various companies, ranging from microchips, for which a large part of the manufacture is carried out under the microscope, to large hydro-electric power generators, electric locomotives and nuclear power stations. In some companies only white collar workers are employed. However, this case study is chiefly concerned with manual workers. The fact that the manufacturing process is so extraordinarily diverse has had a great influence on the innovation process.

Problems such as the motivation to modify procedures
During the 25 year period over which the author has been observing the (ABB) Group, problems with a direct bearing on the employees have been the following:

Absence due to illness, chiefly amongst manual workers, has, in certain companies, increased to an alarming level during this time. In some companies employing between 3,000 and 4,000 manual workers, levels of over 20% sickness absence have been noted. The number of instances of illness which have been accepted and compensated as industrial injuries by the social insurance office has been high, with a preponderance of stress related illnesses of a type which many researchers judged to be largely caused by psychosocial factors. Sickness absence amongst white collar workers has remained consistently at a significantly lower level.

Staff turnover has been high and costly for the company. Naturally it has varied a great deal between the various enterprises in the ABB Group in Sweden, but in certain areas, it has been high enough to lead to significant production problems, brought about by disruption to manufacture, and quality problems caused by inexperienced staff and the high costs of training new employees.

Throughout the 1980's, in particular, employment in industry in Sweden was extraordinarily unpopular. The working conditions offered were not attractive to job seekers. Work in the engineering industry was rated at the bottom of the scale in surveys carried out amongst young people on the subject of the careers they wished to follow. Efforts were made to counter this attitude through propaganda, but the majority of young people who began working in industry gave up again within a few months. The problem was not principally the physical working environment but simply the organization of work, involving simple, undemanding tasks requiring no self-motivation and lacking any opportunity to make full use of their capabilities.

All these personnel problems naturally had a direct effect on production. The quality of products deteriorated. Throughput times for products, which of course entail considerable economic consequences, grew longer and the level of service, meaning the number of products delivered within a given time, became worryingly low, which in turn resulted in the loss of customers.

The predominant medical problem of the working environment

The greatest medical problem was stress related illness in which, as has been mentioned, nervous tension of increasing magnitude was a strong causal factor. The company doctor realised as early as the beginning of the 1970's that these illnesses needed to be prevented through a combination of ergonomics, automation and changes to work organization. It was the intention that this last innovation should add some variety to work tasks in addition to varying muscle stress, as well as introducing meaningful, self-motivated work with a substantial and enriching content.

It was relatively easy to obtain the sympathy of the corporate management for the first two of the above mentioned innovations and modification procedures were activated within the various ABB companies concerned.

The idea of modifying the organization of work through job enlargement and enrichment, and the organization of objective-oriented work groups, was also accepted by the senior management. The company doctor who promoted these ideas obtained support and encouragement for his continued efforts. The management's support for this was intellectual, but neither unanimous nor wholehearted. The innovation process was not given priority over other important tasks, and over a period of about 15 years there was only a very slow relaxation of the Taylorist organization of work. The innovation procedures did not come into effect with any force.

A breakthrough for the innovation process

It often needs a combination of several factors for a major process of innovation to be set in motion. This was the case with ABB, and not least within a small department in one of the companies. The innovation process described later in this case study soon proved to be very successful and came to be seen as a model for other companies within the Group to emulate.

The target group

Approximately 50 people, mainly women, were working within this department at the time. The department manufactured relatively simple electrical products. However, the manufacturing process involved a large number of variant parts and had to be constantly adaptable in order to meet the clients' requirements. The work tasks ran in short cycles, were monotonous, lacking in stimulus or responsibility and devoid of any opportunity for development.

The Problems

In 1988, sickness absence in this department represented 35% of the available working time and staff turnover was 39%. The costs of diminished production resulting from these high levels and of training new staff amounted to as much as 3.8 million Swedish Krone (almost ECU 400,000) in 1988. A day's absence through illness is reckoned to cost 1,000 Swedish Krone (ECU 105) and training of new employees 70,000 Swedish Krone (ECU 7,350). The calculation process which produced this key figure was very instructive.

The substantial personnel problems were also reflected in the production process. There was a worryingly high quantity of 'goods in progress'. The throughput time from order to delivery was 12 days, which was judged to be far too long for so simple a product. The level of service, meaning the number of products delivered to the customer within the agreed time, was 25%. Because of these poor results, there was a perceived threat that manufacturing could be transferred to some other company within ABB's worldwide organization.

A combination of factors

In 1988, a number of different factors combined to bring about far-reaching changes:
Statistics relating to the occurrence of stress related injuries were compiled and revealed alarmingly high percentages. The high costs of absence through illness and staff turnover had been brought to the fore in a very effective way through an energetic debate in the mass media. Similar costs had been calculated and reported by ABB on previous occasions, but had never had any impact other than being recorded and filed away. Through the active debate which now began, people were made aware of the costs, which featured permanently as a vivid, topical factor in the discussions. At the same time, ABB appointed a new

production expert who was inspired by the desire to create a new form of work organization. During this period, it had also become possible to use economic resources from a special public fund to implement this innovation process. In addition, the relevant industrial safety engineer had been trained in issues relating to the psychosocial work environment and processes of innovation within the work environment. Furthermore, the trade union had given priority status to the issue of a good psychosocial work environment. And undoubtedly most important of all, ABB in Sweden had acquired a Group Managing Director who understood not only intellectually but also intuitively the importance of introducing new parameters for meaningful work in the engineering industry.

There arose therefore simultaneously:-

* a clear crisis mentality
* an understanding of the economic consequences
* a committed leader for the cause of innovation (i.e. the production expert)
* a skilled "consultant" (i.e. the safety engineer)
* economic support for the innovation scheme
* strong support from the trade union
* strong support from senior management

INTERVENTION

The innovation strategy

The aim of the innovation strategy was to create independent work groups which could take over responsibility for a substantial part of the production process. As the amount of 'work in hand' varied greatly depending on which type of product was to be manufactured, there was a need for considerable flexibility in order to attain the necessary flows more rapidly and to provide the customer with better service.

In order to attain flexibility, the staff needed to be trained to acquire broader skills, and the basis for planning the 'new work organization' was for maximum skills development. This goal was also intended to provide the variety and improvement to the psychosocial work environment, which the company health service was pleading for. The aim of training everybody to their full capabilities to manage a product throughout the entire production process is often a Utopian ideal, and in the case in point it was possible to divide the tasks into 6 groups, of which three could be said to constitute a goal which everyone needed to attain. The remaining three - material planning, quality matters and the co-ordination of the group's work - represented a voluntary "superstructure", to which the most competent and ambitious could aspire.

Developing skills

Training to achieve broader occupational proficiency was carried out on the master/apprentice model, with an experienced work colleague acting as teacher. This method proved to have many advantages compared with formal courses: (1) a work colleague will know precisely which skills are needed at his own workplace; (2) there is the opportunity for training during quiet periods; (3) a work colleague "talks the same language" as his pupil; (4) is still there at the workplace after the training has finished; (5) can help the pupil to exploit his skills in a practical way at work during the course of the training; and above all, (6) being trained by a work colleague means that the person doing the teaching acquires great self-esteem. The importance of this last factor cannot be exaggerated.

Alongside the purely occupational training there were training programmes in a number of overlapping areas relating to the company: economics, quality matters, design, sales, problem solving methodology, and many other topics. These training courses were run by members of staff for employees in their own company. In this way a greater understanding of the role of an employee's particular area of production was obtained in relation to the company as a whole, thereby creating a greater sense of kinship.

Alongside these courses there was also training by external consultants in conflict management, group dynamics, relationship psychology and other so-called "soft" issues, the intention being to ensure that the work in the groups would flow well.

In an effort to see that everyone would participate in the groups' active involvement in production planning, implementation of skills development, working with continuous improvements, and so on, the company also invested in a two-day training course in 'presentation skills'. The number of group members who were shy, passive and silent was probably greatly reduced as a result of this training.

Vertical work enrichment

By virtue of the group members' improved skills and the simplification of many routine procedures, it became possible for the employees to take over responsibility for many of the tasks traditionally carried out by management. Work was distributed within the group, overtime allocated as required, new members of staff trained, materials procured, repairs commissioned, contact established with other departments in the company, and the basis for wages justified, etc.

The wage system

The wage system was modified. Previously there had been an individual agreement in the group. Now a wage system was devised comprising a fixed part and flexible part, the latter being dependent on the group's results and calculated on the basis of productivity, quality and prompt deliveries. The flexible part was distributed equally amongst the group.

The Results

The innovation process was introduced in 1990 and is still going on. New areas for improvement are continually being found. A follow up study was carried out in 1991 and the results were compared with those of 1988. The findings for the department can be seen in the table below.

Table 2.1 : Main Results of the Innovation Process

	1988	1991
Throughput time	12 days	1.5 days
Staff turnover	39%	0%
Level of service	25%	98%
Absence through illness (excluding long term occupational injury and illness)	14%	4%
Stock index (stock and work in progress)	100%	114%
* Long term occupational injury and illness cases	35	0
* Musculo-skeletal injuries (whole company)	255 cases	10 cases (1994)

Notes: cost of one sickleave day = 1000 Swedish Krone
* not directly comparable 1988-1991 because of changes in sickness/disability insurance

Profitability

Profitability figures were calculated for the department. The costs of absence through illness and staff turnover together with the effects of savings achieved in 'stock' and 'goods in progress' resulted in a 12% reduction in production costs. *The annual saving amounted to 1.5 million Swedish Krone (ECU 157,500 approximately). The costs of the intervention* in terms of training, lost production time and workplace improvement costs similarly *amounted to 1.5 million Swedish Krone (ECU 157,500).* Therefore the interventions paid for themselves within one year.

Word spreads throughout the Group

This success story, which gained a lot of attention and a great deal of media coverage, was instrumental in the implementation of a programme which, not without reason, has been dubbed a cultural revolution and which has now been launched within the Group. The scheme is called T50. The psychology, which is an integral part of this innovation process, is particularly instructive. "T" stands for the concept of time and "50" relates to the idea that the average time taken from 'order to delivery' in the Group should be reduced by 50%. It is intended that this should happen within three years. The same target is to be applied to design procedures, for instance, as well. Reducing throughput times in this way was nothing new; the Group Board of Management had stressed the importance of this for decades. But two other very important details were added.

Clear definition of objectives
The goal of "time reduction" was what had always been targeted in the past. The reason was, of course, that the time reduction which might be possible varied greatly from process to process. The new Group management formulated a simple, easily understandable average objective which all employees could identify in their own environment. Everyone could interpret this as a challenge to contribute towards attaining that goal.

No precise guidance as to methods
The second difference was that there was no definition of the methods which should be applied to attain the objective. In other companies it had been observed how management had defined the training courses for different hierarchical groupings, the consultants, the timescale etc., thus making it unnecessary for each company to "invent the wheel". This hampered creativity and motivation. The ABB Group in Sweden comprises companies with very different types of production - the micro sector, locomotives, large-scale generators, service products, etc. - which is why it was meaningless to try to direct in every detail. Instead of this approach, it was emphasised that every company, division and department should find its own ways of achieving the goal.

A "toolbox" was devised containing methods which could be applied to do the job. It contained a thoroughly prepared personnel policy, methods for achieving continuous improvements, skills development, flexibility, objective-oriented groups, benchmarking, activity-based cost monitoring etc. A small staff group was appointed as a support for the companies, other companies were visited and ideas derived from them, a series of seminars was arranged in which senior management always took part and which, perhaps because of this, was extremely well patronised. Very soon more and more successful examples within the Group were identified and were able to demonstrate their strategies for success at the seminars. Senior management exploited every possibility to demonstrate clearly its strength of interest in work organization that was new, more stimulating and at the same time more efficient. This was done in the absolute conviction that the new form of work organization was the most supremely effective means of attaining the goal of more efficient production through which to increase competitiveness.

The Results of the Group

The aim of the T50 programme was a time reduction of 50% over 3 years, which was a very challenging goal. When the results were monitored, a figure of 47% was found, which was totally acceptable.

The results in terms of sickness absence and staff turnover are difficult to define for many reasons. One reason is that the Group comprises many independent companies with their own statistics, which are not compiled to produce a single figure at any time. Furthermore, a prolonged, deep recession coincided with the innovations. Another reason is that many changes in health insurance arrangements were introduced during this period, including a qualifying period, reduced compensation payments, and the payment of benefits by the employer for the first two weeks. This influenced the sickness absence rate, which has consistently dropped in a very dramatic way.

The near-disappearance of stress-related injury

One figure, not influenced by the changes in regulations, was the number of notified cases of stress-related injury, which was monitored very carefully in the company in Vasteras. Here there was a reduction of 91.7% (225 cases notified in 1988; 19 in 1994). This result, which has been used as an example for particular scientific investigation, has been described as very remarkable. Numerous companies within the Group are reporting great success in the areas such as level of service, quality, tied-up capital, etc.

The importance of the methods rather than the goal

A biography of Steve Jobs, the creator of Macintosh, is entitled "The Journey is the Reward". This could very well have been applied to the T50 programme.

In order to attain the goal, measures of such magnitude were taken in different companies within the Group that there was talk of an industrial revolution. From the starting point of a Taylorist type of organization, employees' skills were developed and work enrichment and variety introduced. It was found that even poorly educated, older employees, who had been doing repetitive, monotonous work for decades, possessed a great 'development potential'. It was found that, with skills development and support, it was possible to delegate many decisions to the vicinity of the production line. Almost everywhere it was found that an organization with strong, independent, objective-oriented groups was the route which led to the goal and in 1994 it was estimated that about 1,000 objective-oriented groups had been formed within the ABB Group.

The significance of the scheme for employees

Positive efforts were made to carry out systematic and uniform surveys at the beginning of the innovation process, with the intention of repeating this procedure in a similar fashion in all the companies within the Group some years later. The initial values were extremely low. Amongst engineering workers about one in three or four thought that work was managed efficiently, that their skills were utilised, that there was a good team spirit, and that it was possible to influence one's working conditions, etc. Many managers found the negative attitudes depressing. Others, however, perceived that there was great potential for improvement, taking the attitude: "If we can participate in a competitive market when we have such poor practices, we should be able to become world-beaters if we can improve."

Follow-up surveys have been carried out in different companies but there has not been any uniform compilation allowing an ongoing comparison to be made, nor could there have been, since the investigations were not uniform themselves. In many companies the improvement in attitudes was dramatic; in others it has amounted to a moderate success; but taken overall, improvements have been visible. The reasons for the lack of a serious, uniform scientific investigation may be that everyone is agreed as to the enormous benefit of the changes which have taken place. Everyone is continuing with the tasks of improving further the decentralised organization of work, and there will be no turning back to Taylorism. In a technically oriented company like ABB, there is little interest in becoming bogged down in analysis.

The author has systematically interviewed many people at all hierarchical levels in the Group, making hundreds of contacts with different individuals, and has never encountered anything other than highly positive reactions to the innovation process. Not infrequently the individuals questioned have testified to a touching improvement in the quality of life of particular employees.

Stress prevention and profitability

The changes in work organization which have been described above can well be said to come under the heading of stress prevention. Attempts have been made by staff members within the Group to evaluate these changes in monetary terms. Profitability has in fact shown itself in terms of reduced levels of 'capital tied up in stock' and 'work in progress'. Productivity has been made more efficient through more 'flexible flows', making it possible, without working any faster, to produce more with the existing workforce. More up-to-date designs has been put on the market more quickly, which can of course mean a significant competitive advantage. Almost all products are now delivered to the customer within the agreed time, which was not the case previously, and the value of this cannot be overestimated, although it is difficult to express it in Krone.

All these positive merits, which have an extremely significant impact on the bottom line, are the result of many accumulated contributions, none of which can be isolated and categorised as stress prevention. The following aspects represent factors which affect the individual's psychosocial work environment in a very positive way, and which at the same time have an undeniably favourable effect on production: delegation of responsibility, skills development, broader and deeper responsibility, information, dialogue between employers and employees, the freedom to plan, and the power to influence goals.

Case Study II

Nelissen Van Egteren Bouw Heerlen BV

This study reports on the effects of an integrated health promotion programme introduced in a small division of a Dutch construction company. The intervention was designed to improve the consultative structure within the organization and provide managerial skills training in the area of communication, stress recognition and stress management to enable managers to more sensitively and effectively handle stress in themselves and their subordinates. Although the training programme focused on construction site managers, the benefits associated with the programme extended across the whole company and had a significant impact in reducing the incidence of sickness absence.

The main points illustrated by the case study are:-

- the importance of diagnostic activity, to identify organization-specific problems and guide the intervention strategy, and in providing baseline data by which to evaluate its effectiveness. In this case, questionnaire and interview data were collected
- the importance of establishing comparable control groups
- the importance of establishing the attitudes of organizational members towards stress intervention strategies. In this case, 65% of middle management expressed their willingness to participate in this type of programme
- in the period 1992-1994 the overall level of sickness absence declined by more than 30% compared to the control group. One third of this decline was ascribed to the intervention programme itself
- the financial savings which resulted were more than sufficient to cover the programme costs and yield a surplus
- as with the previous case study, other important benefits occurred which were not directly measurable in economic terms, e.g. improved employee relations and increased motivation

Stress-Related Interventions in Construction Work

Professor Frans Nijhuis, M.L. Lendfers, A. de Jong, P. Janssen and A Ament
University of Limburg, Maastricht, The Netherlands

The average rate of sickness absenteeism for Europe is currently between 1%-2% (CBI - Percon Survey, 1994). A distinctive feature of the Netherlands as compared with other European countries is its rate of sickness absenteeism. Sickness absenteeism in the Netherlands over the years 1988-1991 reached an average of 8 per cent and was much higher than in the UK, where it is 3.5% or Belgium or Germany (Prins, 1990). In this study sickness absenteeism was measured in days per year.

$$\% \text{ sickness absenteeism} = \frac{\text{total sick days (calendar days) for a company}}{N \text{ (number of employees) } *365 \text{ in full time equivalents}} *100$$

In this study sickness absenteeism has a maximum duration of 365 days, because the labour contract of the company with the worker normally stops after 365 days of illness of the worker and the worker may get a disability pension.

Sickness absenteeism is based on full-time equivalents workers.

Increasing absenteeism rates since 1985 and, particularly, correspondingly growing costs (production costs, quality costs, costs of continued payment of wages, and of medical expenses) have led to a great number of absence prevention programmes in Dutch enterprises during the last few years. Most of these programmes have been aimed at improving either the working conditions or the workers' absence behaviour through better control procedures and absence guidance by company doctors and medical advisers of insurance agencies.

Experiences with absence prevention programmes have suggested that to be effective it is necessary to apply an integrated approach of activities aimed at improving the work situation as a whole, the contributions of company doctors and medical advisers, of insurance agencies, and worker values, norms and behaviour. This is in line with recent developments in the field of lifestyle programmes which attempt to influence health behaviour through a combination of rules, training courses and information. Here, too, it can be concluded that prevention is achieved more effectively by applying a combination of integrated absence prevention programmes and lifestyle-oriented programmes. This approach is called an **Integrated Health Promotion Programme.** It is designed to reduce absenteeism by eliminating or minimising workplace health risks and promoting health and well being.

In order to test the integrated health promotion approach in all its facets, the Dutch Ministries of Social Affairs and Employment, Social Welfare and the General Disability Fund commissioned two pilot projects of four years each.

The Target Company

One of the projects was carried out by the Netherlands Organization for Applied Scientific Research (TNO/PG) in the field of healthcare. The other, which was conducted by the University of Limburg, and is the focus of this case study was in the construction industry. It concerns the evaluation of the stress management programme that formed part of the Integrated Health Promotion programme which was introduced in a small construction company in the south of the country. It was selected for the project because of the high risk of absence and disability associated with this particular business sector. The selected company, employs some 150-200 workers. Although part of a national holding company, it operates autonomously and has its own internal policies. The core of its business activities is in building public utilities, i.e. large industrial projects such as water purification plants. Two similar construction companies within the same holding company were designated control companies. Table 2.2 presents an overview of the main staff characteristics of the intervention company and the two control companies at the onset of the project (1992).

Table 2.2 :Staff Characteristics of Intervention and Control Companies

	Intervention company	Control I	Control II
Number of employees:	**145**	**157**	**123**
Building workers	97	102	70
Age categories:			
< 24 years	3	7	5
25-34 years	12	21	16
35-44 years	36	33	19
45-54 years	36	37	25
> 55 years	10	4	5
Engineering/administration	48	55	53
Age categories:			
< 24 years	4	1	1
25-34 years	10	14	8
35-44 years	15	15	20
45-54 years	14	17	22
> 55 years	5	8	2
Sex:			
Male	139	149	110
Female	6	8	13
Termination of employment	21	19	22
Number of accidents (number of days absent due to accident)	13 (278)	10 (275)	5 (273)

Overall, the intervention company and the two control companies appeared to be quite similar.

Organizational Arrangements

Following the initial selection of the intervention company and the two control companies meetings were held with both general managers and staff representatives of all three companies. These discussions resulted in an agreement between the researchers/counsellors and the intervention organization. Next, an internal support committee was established which was made responsible for giving advice on potential projects and their execution. The support committee included representatives of all relevant staff categories.

Analysis of Starting Conditions

The work situation as well as the health and well-being of the workers was examined in three ways. First, absenteeism was analysed for those workers who had been employed throughout the years 1991 and/or 1992. This resulted in the data presented in Table 2.3 This table describes the number of sick-leave cases per (full-time) employee for the construction workers, for the technical and administration personnel and for the total population of the control and intervention organizations.

Table 2.3 Absence data 1991-1992

	Intervention company (n=116)			Control I (n=97)			Control II (n=92)		
	Build.	Tech/Admin	Total	Build.	Tech/Admin	Total	Build.	Tech/Admin	Total
1991 sickness absenteeism									
percentage	11.45	6.3	9.74	10.26	4.00	7.70	12.02	3.91	7.6
frequency	1.54	1.04	1.38	1.30	0.62	1.02	1.32	0.94	1.19
1992 sickness absenteeism									
percentage	11.40	5.3	9.38	9.77	1.94	6.9	11.57	5.55	8.71
frequency	1.56	0.71	1.28	1.27	0.72	1.07	1.24	0.98	1.17

The intervention company generally did not differ from the control companies, either in a positive or negative sense.

Secondly, a broad diagnostic survey was carried out among the employees of both the intervention company and the control companies. The survey addressed the following topics:

- demographic data (age, seniority, sex)
- stressors in the work situation with regard to labour relationships, job contents, and working conditions
- physical and climatological conditions, physical stress in the work situation
- health behaviour (smoking, drinking, exercise, coping)
- complaints about health and well-being

This case study will discuss a small, albeit substantial, part of the entire programme, i.e. the interventions in labour relations which were achieved by applying a broad stress management approach.

Stress at Construction Sites

Construction work evokes a picture of heavy physical labour under varying climatic conditions. Because of its physical conditions, it has long been the focus of attention of researchers in the field of health and labour. However, mental strain is another major problem in construction work, especially for middle managers.

In the Netherlands, as well as in the UK, it has been frequently established over the past few years that it is particularly at middle-management level (i.e. construction managers and site managers) that employees have increased risks of burn-out due to stress-related complaints (Sutherland & Davidson 1993; Offermans et al., 1988; Draaisma, Grundemann and Hoolboom 1991; Grundemann, Draaisma and Hoolboom 1992).

Sources of stress-related complaints include:

- lack of relevant information
- tensions between work planning and necessary resources, including manpower
- tensions between time pressure and quality of work
- lack of management support, and
- inadequate task organization

Working as a middle manager in the building industry differs from being employed in the manufacturing industry. Middle managers in construction work are responsible for the delivery and quality of their building projects according to clearly pre-defined specifications. In operating at a distance from Headquarters, site managers have a great deal of autonomy. Typically, they are able to make decisions about a great many aspects of the building process, e.g. materials to be used; the planning of tasks on site. However, they must adhere to the methods of construction and end terms (date of completion, quality etc.) defined in the contract terms. The task of the site manager is to produce a building with the means at his/her disposal - in accordance with its quality definition, often within extremely tight time constraints.

The Diagnosis (1992)

Following the study design (Figure 2.21) the original situation was analysed by conducting several interviews. These initial data were operationalised in an extensive questionnaire covering a great number of variables, which was presented to each employee in 1992.

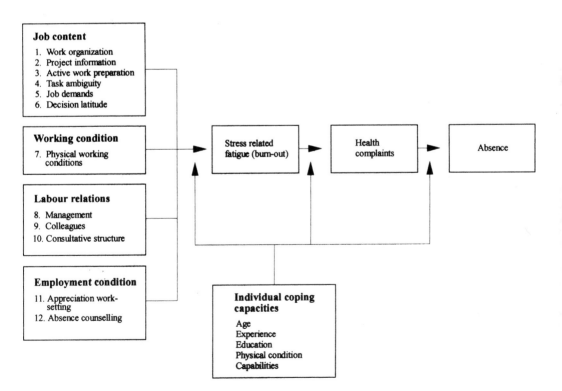

Figure 2.21 Research model

The primary purpose of the questionnaire was to analyse the work situation in terms of health and labour. In the survey stress symptoms were operationalised as fatigue (burn-out). Additional measures included health complaints (self-reported) and absence in annual number of days (administrative data) for all employees during the intervention period.

The survey questionnaire was sent to all employees, inviting them to return the completed form. Their response was high, both in the intervention company and the control companies (see Table 2.4). Thus, the response rates would ensure a representative picture of the beliefs and experiences of the workers in all three of these companies.

Table 2.4. Response Rates

	Mailed (N)	Response (%)
Intervention company	145	80
Control I	157	78
Control II	123	86

Based on the results of this survey and on interviews with key informants it was concluded that the problems in the areas of labour relations (information, consultative structure, comradeship, relations between management and shop-floor workers, participation) and job content (task organization, task-related information, demands and control) were felt to be considerable (Table 2.5).

In its initial phase, therefore, the project was aimed primarily at bringing about changes in labour relations and job content. Furthermore, the middle management level (the construction site manager) appears to play a central role in the building organization. These managers are highly responsible for planning and executing constructions, often at great distances from the head office. For this reason, the analysis of stressors was aimed primarily and exclusively at this category of workers.

Analysis of the Initial Survey

First, the survey was used to examine whether these impressions were correct. The survey offers two possibilities:

1. an analysis of how various job aspects of construction site managers are associated with stress-related fatigue (burn-out)
2. an analysis of how much stress is felt by construction site managers and whether they are prepared to become actively involved in a stress management programme

A correlational analysis of the relations between work, work organization variables and health indices (Figure 2.22) shows that:

- high levels of stress-related fatigue are caused by:
  * how the building project has been organized
  * the information provided on the building project
  * task vagueness
  * relations with management
  * appreciation of the work setting
  * how employees are treated when being sick

- burn-out also appears to be strongly related with subjective health complaints - and subjective health complaints are related with absence.

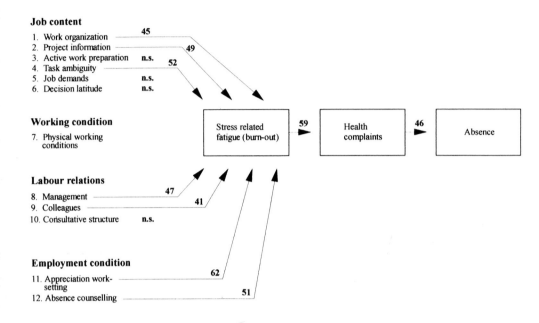

Figure 2.22 Correlations between work and organization variables of construction site managers, burn-out, and absence

In addition, the hypothesized level of subjective work stress among construction site managers proved to be confirmed.

The 1992 survey also showed that 74 % of those employed in middle management experienced some amount of work stress, while 73 % wanted to improve their coping skills in relation to work stress and 65 % would also like to participate in a stress management training course organized by their company. These data confirmed that work stress was felt to be a major problem for this category of workers and the results formed the basis of a broad stress management programme directed at this category of workers.

Two years after the initial measurement, the same survey was carried out once more among the workforce of the same building company (1994). The differences between the two measurements were used to measure any effects of the interventions. Since the interventions focused on middle management, the research questions will refer specifically to this category of workers.

Developing Stress Management Interventions

Within the organization an internal support committee was established. Members of the committee included representatives of the various staff categories in the organization (management, employees, company doctor). The results of the analyses were discussed in this support committee and the committee decided to take the 1992 data as a starting point for carrying out four stress-preventing interventions:

1. **Improvements in the consultative structure,** making it a more structural activity for the various relevant actors to exchange information. Within the context of these consultative structures, arrangements were made regarding competencies and responsibilities at project level.

2. **A training course for middle management** and higher management levels to teach them better **communication skills** (2 days).

3. **A training course in stress management** (2 days) in order to learn how to cope more adequately with stressors in the work situation (planning, time management, increased problem-solving capacity).

4. An **interview training** to teach employees in managerial functions how to deal more adequately with job-related or stressor-related problems of employees (2 days).

The primary aim of the stress interventions has been to prevent stress-related complaints and diseases. The stress interventions seek

1. to foster awareness and recognition of stressors and attendant health effects

2. to enlarge the individual's capacity to change stressful working conditions or to deal with those stressors

3. to train individuals in stress reduction strategies (e.g. Murphy, 1988)

This type of approach seeks to limit any stressors present in the job environment as well as to exert some influence on how workers deal with stressors in their work situation (Figure 2.23).

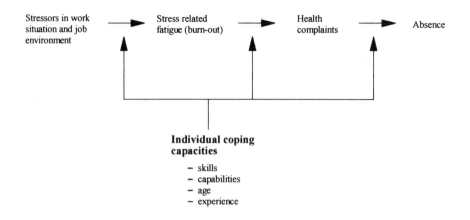

Figure 2.23 Stress versus strength: a revised model (adapted from Van Dijk et al, 1990; see also Israel, Schurman and House, 1989)

The interventions started in the autumn of 1992. Effects of interventions, if any, could therefore be expected to occur during the year 1993.

Research Questions

Two main research questions will be discussed here:

1. to what extent do these stress-related interventions result in a reduction of health complaints and absenteeism?
2. what is the cost-effectiveness of interventions?

The Impact of the Intervention

On the basis of pre and post intervention data (Table 2.5) it can be concluded that considerable improvements have been achieved particularly in the assessment of job elements associated with task organization and consultative structure. This has led to significantly reduced perceptions of stress as emanating from these job aspects (p < .01). No differences could be found regarding physical burden and relations with higher management levels.

Table 2.5 Changes in work-related variables (1992 vs. 1994)

Variables	Survey 1992	Survey 1994	p	Direction of change
Job Contents				
1. Work organization	.45	.26	.001	fewer complaints
2. Project information	.78	.58	.045	fewer complaints
3. Active work preparation	.50	.11	.002	fewer complaints
4. Task ambiguity	2.32	1.98	.007	fewer complaints
5. Job demands	.72	.61	.023	fewer complaints
6. Decision latitude	.19	.11	ns	----
Working Conditions				
7. Physical working conditions	.04	.08	ns	-----
Labour Relations				
8. Relationships with management	.36	.30	.084	fewer complaints
9. Relations with colleagues	.51	.34	.006	fewer complaints
10. Consultative structure	.44	.22	.001	fewer complaints
Employment Conditions				
11. Appreciation work setting	.31	.29	ns	-----
12. Absence counselling	.62	.18	.002	fewer complaints
Stress related fatigue	2.79	2.69	ns	-----
Health complaints	5.50	4.69	ns	-----

Managerial absence also decreased over the two year period. This reduction appeared to be considerable in comparison with control groups (i.e. in similar building companies).

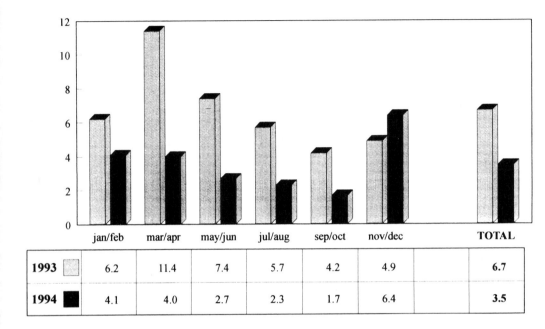

		jan/feb	mar/apr	may/jun	jul/aug	sep/oct	nov/dec		TOTAL
1993		6.2	11.4	7.4	5.7	4.2	4.9		**6.7**
1994		4.1	4.0	2.7	2.3	1.7	6.4		**3.5**

Figure 2.24 Sickness absenteeism work-site management (%)

Cost Effectiveness of the Intervention Programme

The cost effectiveness of the stress management programme is not only expressed in gains that are directly observable, for example, reduced absenteeism. There have been important benefits to the whole organization in:-

- educating employees in detecting stress related complaints and teaching them to seek assistance if necessary;

- higher motivation as a result of reduced feelings of stress and discontent as well as greater efforts to deliver a high-quality performance

- improved relations with co-workers

- greater capacity for spotting and solving any problems. It was one of the objectives of the intervention to teach site managers that it is not a show of incompetence to point out potential problems and that others are usually faced with similar problems. They were also made aware that they were supposed to solve many problems at the site independently

These are important elements of a cost effective stress management programme.

Thus, the benefits can be expressed in several advantages which will be discussed below in more detail. They are:

1. cost reduction through reduced absenteeism of construction site managers

2. greater capacity for spotting and solving problems

3. improved efforts by workers at the building site

1. Cost reduction through reduced absence

In the Netherlands, workers' wages continue to be paid during their time of illness, up to a maximum period of 12 months. At the end of this period, they become eligible for disability benefits. As a rule, Dutch enterprises have joint, branch-specific insurance for the wage costs to be paid in case of illness (sickness benefits). Companies have to pay for the first six weeks of their workers' sick leave - and a limited extra allowance on top of subsequent sickness benefits.

Absence in the study sample decreased by 30%. Prior to the intervention, the annual average rate of sickness absence amongst construction managers and site managers was 15 days. This has reduced to 10 days. Apart from the direct benefits to the organization (no replacement costs etc), there have been indirect cost reductions and benefits in that building projects have been less disrupted.

2. Greater capacity for spotting and solving problems

At the start of the intervention project, job-related or organizational problems were considered to be insoluble ('that's how it is in construction industry, you just have to live with it') or they were passed on to higher management levels. Since the interventions began, an active problem solving attitude has developed within the organization. Workers will raise problems with the management, but they will also seek their own solutions. Many of the problems that are brought to the attention of the organization in this way can now be solved as a result of improved information and consultation during the preparation, start and execution of the building project. As a result, this has led to increasing pressure within the organization to alter its internal consultative structure. Also, since the intervention workers now apply different approaches to their workplace problems because they are better informed and have greater participation in setting policies regarding working conditions and health and safety issues.

Another measurable outcome of the training was its impact on the 'locus of control' scores of the managers. After having completed the stress management course, the site managers felt that they had more control and influence over their own health and were less "externally" controlled. The organization is now planning a training course for all its employees to improve discussions on how things are going on the shop-floor.

These types of changes will not only result in direct cost benefits, but more importantly, will certainly lead to improved motivation, less disruption at the workplace and the prevention of absence and stress related complaints.

3.   Improved efforts by workers at the building site

The closer attention which middle managers now pay in recognising and pointing out stress related problems has resulted in their dealing more adequately with both their own stress related complaints and those of their employees. This is shown, for example, in a marked increase in the workers' appreciation of consultative procedures and the ways in which immediate line managers deal with their workers' absence. In addition, there has been a marked drop in absence rates (from approximately 10% in 1991 to 8% in 1993) for the total population (Figure 2.25). This latter development exceeds the decline in the control companies by more than 30%.

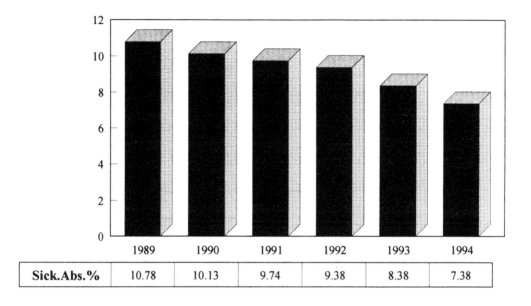

| Sick.Abs.% | 10.78 | 10.13 | 9.74 | 9.38 | 8.38 | 7.38 |

Figure 2.25 Sickness absenteeism total population (%)

A multiple regression analysis was used to examine how (experienced) differences in stressors (social relations, task information, improved organization, and participation) might explain possible differences in individual absence rates. The regression analysis demonstrated that 34% of the individual decrease in absence rates could be explained by differences in assessments between measurements 1 and 2.

Thus, in view of the amount of explained variance in this regression analysis, 34% of the difference in absence rates between 1990-1992 and 1993-1994 can be attributed to the interventions. This would imply that, on a total reduction of 780 days of absence for the construction workers in 1993, the interventions have been responsible for a reduction of 260 days. The year 1994 had a total of 825 fewer days of absence; 275 of them can be explained by the observed differences.

Economic evaluation of the intervention programme

In economic evaluation the costs of the programme has to be compared with the benefits of the programme. The costs of the programme are fairly easy to calculate based on the respective inputs of the programme. The benefits are much harder to assess, because it is not always obvious how to validate the different effects. Such an economic evaluation can be performed from different points of view: the enterprise, the government or the whole society. Below the costs and benefits of such a programme will be assessed merely from the point of view of the individual enterprise. However some clues will be presented with regard to the societal impact of the programme.

The costs of the programme

The intervention consists of three separate components: there was an absence counselling programme, a training course for middle management and a course on stress management. Furthermore, there was an organizational support committee (preparing actions, analysing the results etc.) and its time will have to be taken into account. In Table 2.6 the number of hours and the money spent per component are represented.

Table 2.6 : Costs of intervention

	Number of hours	Income per hour	Costs
1. Committee of supervision (5 meetings of 2 hours)			
Participants : 4 middle managers	40	f 65,-	f 2,600,-
3 construction workers	30	f 47,50	f 1.425,-
2. Absence counselling (2 meetings of 4 hours)			
Participants: 20 middle managers	160	f 65,-	f 10.400,-
Programme costs			f 7.500,-
3. Training middle managers (in total 12 hours)			
Participants: 24 middle managers	288	f 65,-	f 18.720,-
Programme costs			f 15.000,-
4. Stress management (in total 12 hours)			
Participants: 24 middle managers	288	f 65,-	f 18.720,-
Programme costs			f 30.000,-
Total costs			f 104.360,-

The total costs of the implementation of such a programme amount to f 100.000 (Table 2.6), i.e. approximately ECU 48,000.. Almost 50% of this amount is needed for the component stress management. About 50% of the costs consists of lost production of the participants of the courses. The associated costs are obtained by multiplying the hours by the average hourly wages. This is explained in more detail in the discussion section.

The benefits of the programme

The possible effects of such a programme are very diverse. Primarily, the programme was aimed at reducing absenteeism amongst the middle managers. Furthermore, it was expected that it would have some secondary effects, namely the reduction of absenteeism of construction workers as a result of improved functioning of the middle management. Additionally, it was expected that the quality of the whole organizational functioning would be improved, through anticipating emerging problems. It is very difficult to assess the value of these rather qualitative organizational aspects. Therefore, these aspects can not be taken into account in the cost-benefit analysis.

In Table 2.7 the two first mentioned effects are quantified by using the same method for calculating the costs. The determination of the benefits is performed as follows. In the first place the average percentage of absenteeism for each professional category is determined for the years 1993 and 1994. During these years the percentage of absenteeism declined. The decline was more than 30% higher than the decline in the control companies, and the regression analysis showed that the attitudinal effects of the intervention explains 34% of the total decline of the absenteeism. That is why one-third of this decline has been ascribed to the intervention programme itself. The other two-thirds may be caused by nationwide trends in absenteeism. Based on these figures the benefits of the programme can be determined by taking into account the number of workers in different categories and the level of average income per category (Table 2.7).

Table 2.7 : Benefits of the programme

	No. of workers	No. of reduced days absenteeism	Attributed to intervention	Income per day	Benefits overall	Benefits for organization 50%
1993						
Middle managers	24	108	36	ƒ 520,-	ƒ 18.720,-	
Construction workers	130	780	260	ƒ 380,-	ƒ 98.800,-	
Total					ƒ 117.520,-	
1994						
Middle managers	24	160	53	ƒ 520,-	ƒ 27.560,-	
Construction workers	130	825	275	ƒ 380,-	ƒ 104.500	
Improved problem solving capacity					p.m.	p.m.
Improved motivation of the workforce					p.m.	p.m.
Improved relation with colleagues and management					p.m.	p.m.
Less failure through improved information					p.m.	p.m.
Total benefits					ƒ 132.060,-	ƒ 66.039,-
Total benefits 1993-94					ƒ 249.080,-	ƒ 124.540,-

The benefits of the rather qualitative aspects of the organizational improvement are not quantified in the above benefits. The decline in absenteeism of construction workers has a greater effect than the decline in absenteeism of the construction site managers. Furthermore, it can be seen from the table that the total programme costs are earned back within one year. It is important to note that in the Dutch Social Security System the costs of sickness absenteeism will be partially reimbursed by the Social Security Funds. This implies that both the individual companies and the social security funds will profit from the intervention. It may be estimated that at least 50% of the gain of the intervention falls to the organization additional expenses due to replacement costs, overtime costs, salary supplementation, pension contributions, continued pay during absence etc.). The minimal gain for the organization will therefore be 50% of ƒ 250.000, Dutch guilders (approximately ECU 120,000) (Table 2.6). Investing in such programmes can be a very lucrative activity for an enterprise.

The time needed for a stress management programme to yield a surplus to the organization will also depend on the current national social security system. As organizations are increasingly directly accountable for the costs involved in sickness and disablement, it will take less time for interventions to become cost-effective.

DISCUSSION

One of the main problems involved in assessing interventions in actual practice is the distortion of outcomes as a result of:
- self-selection by the intervention company
- the possibility that observed effects cannot be attributed to the intervention (Hawthorne effect)

Self-selection may be a problem if, for example, the company has a deviating pattern of absenteeism. High absence rates due to illness are more easily addressed than low levels of absenteeism; a great number of accidents is easier to reduce than a small number of accidents. However, a comparison of the intervention company with two other construction firms within the same holding company showed that the intervention company did not essentially differ from the two control companies.

It can be assumed, therefore, that the validity of the observed results also applies to other businesses than this particular intervention company.

Nor should the other problem, (i.e. the possibility of a Hawthorne effect) be underestimated; when improvements in consultative structures, changes of style and management, participation, and paying attention to the interests of the workers are implemented, the existing organizational culture will change as well. Paying more attention to the workers could in itself have resulted in a higher level of overall satisfaction - and thus the observed outcome. In that case it would not have been the stress management programme which brought about these changes: any employee-oriented activity might have had the same results.

However, the Hawthorne effect seems less likely because positive job attitudes failed to be found on all job characteristics. For example, no changes occurred in the workers' appreciation of physical stress. It appeared that on those aspects that were not the target of interventions (working conditions, terms of employment, hygiene) the workers' beliefs did not show any positive changes. At the same time, however, it must be concluded that the opinions of construction workers and work-site management did show positive adjustments on the variables related with the actual interventions. What has been taking place, apparently, is a highly specific effect on labour relations rather than overall adjustments.

Some years from now we will be able to determine on the basis of future interventions and studies whether the observed results have taken root. Anyway, for the present it seems that it will not take long before the organization will have recovered its substantial investments in the stress management programme. And the benefits will grow considerably if positive developments continue in 1995. As far as we can see right now, there has not been any relapse into old absenteeism patterns or previous absence rates in 1995. Considering the government's plans to make employers increasingly accountable for the costs of sickness absence it will only become more profitable to invest in promoting the health of workers in the years to come.

The calculation of costs and benefits of such a programme is not without problems. Some of these problems will be discussed below. In the first place there is the problem of how to value absenteeism. From a strictly economic point of view, it is important to assess the real production losses caused by absenteeism. The economic losses depend among others on the category of labour. If absenteeism is relatively short, production loss of middle management is probably very low. For construction workers production loss might show up rather immediately. For longer periods of absenteeism, a construction worker might be substituted more easily than a middle manager. Empirical studies have suggested that the real production losses caused by absenteeism result in lower real costs than suggested by average income of the workers, sometimes less than 10%. In this respect the above mentioned costs and benefits are to be considered as rather tentative. There is another important aspect in evaluating costs and benefits of such a programme. The production losses determine to a great extent the costs as well as the benefits of the intervention. If the methodology used to assess the benefits of the intervention overestimates the benefits, then it must be concluded that the costs may also be overestimated. It follows that the conclusion that such a programme is highly profitable might be unchanged.

Case Study III

Zeneca Pharmaceuticals

This case study forms a report by the Chief Medical Officer on the stress management activities of a large British pharmaceutical company. During the period 1988-1993, almost 700 employees have attended 'in-house' stress management workshops and the Zeneca model has been adopted in other parts of the business. Whilst no direct cost-benefit analysis of the intervention has been conducted, self-report measures of general health show significant improvements post intervention. The number of referrals to psychiatric help/counselling have also decreased.

The main points of the case study illustrate:

- commitment to the activity at the highest level within the organization as a key factor in legitimising the intervention and making it a highly visible and high profile activity

- pre/post intervention measures of general health show an improvement across the total population of 15%-20% some 2-3 months after the workshops

- most importantly, Zeneca's enthusiastic continuance of the programme and its strong endorsement by its Chief Executive, demonstrates that it is not necessary to conduct an economic cost-benefit analysis for senior management to be convinced of its positive value

- for knowledge based industries like Zeneca, with a predominantly white collar workforce, the negative consequences of stress at work have significantly greater implications for employee creativity and decision-making capabilities than absence costs. It would seem that they have recognised that for them to maintain competitive edge, avoiding the problems of "presenteeism" is as important as reducing absenteeism.

Stress Management within the Pharmaceutical Industry
Dr Eric Teasdale, Group Medical Officer, Zeneca, UK

1. Introduction

Zeneca Pharmaceuticals is a large organization. The dimensions, characteristics and "mission" statement of this business are described. This will allow the activities displayed to be put in context. On 1 January 1993, ICI's Pharmaceuticals business together with the Agrochemicals and Seeds and Specialities Business became the constituent members of ZENECA Limited. On 1 June 1993 ZENECA was demerged from ICI and became a separate public limited Company. "New" ICI now consists of the remaining international businesses, namely Paints, Industrial Chemicals, Materials, Explosives and Tioxide Ltd.

In terms of **DIMENSIONS**, sales and trading profits from the Pharmaceuticals business in 1994 were £1,958 million and £629 million respectively. Its products were sold in 130 countries. Manufacturing took place in 17 countries and 13,000 people are involved in the total operations. Research and development "spend" amounted to approximately £260 million per annum.

In terms of **GEOGRAPHICAL SPREAD**, of the 13,000 employed in the Business, 4,400 work in the UK, 3,500 in Continental Western Europe, 2,800 in USA, 800 in Japan and 1,500 in territories located in the rest of the world. By function, 4,700 are involved in Sales and Marketing, 3,600 in Manufacturing, 3,300 in Research and Development and 1,400 in Administration.

It is essential for any organization to define clearly the main areas of activity and thereby target resources appropriately. The "Mission" of ZENECA Pharmceuticals is "To contribute to human health by providing worthwhile products which enable the business to grow and the people in it to prosper and lead fulfilling lives". An enormous amount of work is going into the research and development of new medicines and the current objective is to bring one new product through to launch each year. To achieve this and to ensure that the established business thrives, it is essential to have a 'healthy' organization. This implies having healthy people who are motivated and clearly focused on the job in hand. Ultimately the success of the business depends on the people in it.

2.   Health and Stress

What is HEALTH? It has been defined in many ways. Amongst them are:

> **"a state of complete physical, mental and social well-being, not merely the absence of disease or infirmity"**

> **".......a personal experience of positive enjoyment of life"**

In the occupational or industrial setting, the emphasis on maintaining **mental** (as well as physical and social) well-being is essential to success. In occasional serious cases mental illness must be recognised and managed appropriately. This should include the care of the individual who has a problem of substance abuse, (e.g. alcohol or drugs of addiction), and the patient with a psychotic condition where prompt admission to hospital is required. In practice, however, the more common mental health problems encompass stress, anxiety and depression and their manifestation in the workplace.

The head of ICI/ZENECA Pharmaceuticals Occupational Health function had attended a workshop on stress which took place in Manchester in 1985. Interest in stress-related psychiatric illness had been heightened for some time. There was a fundamental problem in the delivery of mental health care in England which has arisen largely as a result of historical accident. Skills, experience and resources have been concentrated in acute psychiatric hospitals where teams of specialised staff essentially wait for patients to become sufficiently ill to be referred for treatment. Psychiatric care is still stigmatised in England, and the need for psychiatric referral in itself produces stress. The threshold for referral into such care is unrealistically high. Illnesses become unnecessarily severe and patients often wait an unreasonably long time before receiving help. For clinical, humane and economic reasons it would seem appropriate in an enlightened society to embark on preventive psychiatry and to aim to detect and treat disturbance at an earlier stage.

A variety of presentations ranging from the academic to the philosophical were given, but all presenters were obsessed with the definition of stress and the sociological and political issues related to its causation. Suggestions and models for stress management presented were idiosyncratic, fragmented and reflected more the preoccupations of the various stress management consultants, rather than any planned or comprehensive approach. As a result of this, a major piece of work was established to assess the problem within ICI/ZENECA Pharmceuticals and to develop suitable responses.

The motivation for action in ICI/ZENECA resulted from a steadily increasing referral load of known stress related illness. It was understood that many employees conceal their stress related illness from their managers, fearing that they may be seen as weak or as poor prospects for promotion and increased responsibility. These attitudes persist despite evidence to the contrary, and as a result the number of cases known to any company will only ever be the tip of an iceberg of unknown size. Zeneca Pharmaceuticals is a sophisticated and caring employer and was committed to the development of a comprehensive service for Mental as well as Physical Health.

3.   Understanding and Quantifying the Problem

There was obvious concern about the casualty rate and general acceptance that the organization was experiencing high stress levels which were damaging for many individuals.

In common with most, if not all, Occupational Health Departments for large organizations, ZENECA received large amounts of unsolicited materials relating to stress management and was also aware of the existence of employee assistance programmes. These commercially available stress management packages were in their infancy in the UK in 1986, and those available were clearly incomplete, overpriced or unethical - sometimes all three.

A quotation from novelist Alison Lurie is particularly relevant:
> "......and their courses to be composed of equal parts of common sense and nonsense,
> that is, of the already obvious and the probably false"

4. Why not buy an Employee Assistance Programme (EAP)?

EAP's have been an established part of the US employment culture. In essence, they provide confidential counselling usually on site, funded by the employer and conducted either by trained in-house staff or by external consultants. The EAP industry grew rapidly within the US, peaking in the mid 1980's. It was then a predictable and well researched activity which claimed to have demonstrated good cost benefits at an American take-up rate of approximately six employees per thousand per annum. The industry developed haphazardly in the UK, originally by the transplantation into Europe of EAP's which had been home grown by American parent organizations. It is noteworthy that EAP's originally grew out of alcoholism treatment in the US; the identification and management of addictions is still a major focus.

Early UK experience suggested that EAPs were perceived differently by English employees who take up the service more readily, but often with social, domestic or financial problems rather than addictions or psychological distress. Traditionally, English employers have not needed to involve themselves actively in the health care of their employees, leaving such provision to the National Health Service and latterly to Private Health Care funded by private health insurance schemes. Every UK resident is entitled to the services of an NHS family doctor without payment for a service and the traditional EAP model does not sit comfortably alongside existing services. For these and other reasons, ICI/ZENECA in common with many major UK employers had chosen not to follow the EAP model.

5. Internal Research

The Pharmaceuticals industry is undoubtedly an extremely competitive sector in which to operate and much exposed to pressure - which can translate itself into high levels of stress on individuals. It is largely research-orientated, depending on a high degree of creativity with long periods of uncertainty as to the final outcome of expensive development programmes. Such factors compound the pressure on individuals. Tight control of costs, a high volume of new work, the drive for high quality and compliance with Regulatory Authority requirements and the law all make the working environment tough and demanding. In addition to lost time, if employees are under excessive and prolonged pressures for too long, this can lead to an increased incidence of unsafe working practices and accidents in the workplace. There can also be a loss of "creative edge". Poor performance and low morale may also result.

Most organizations may provide no more than a casualty service involving nurses and/or occupational physicians who recognise casualties and deal with them appropriately. It is, we believe, essential to have a positive strategy to manage stress, make it a subject for legitimate discussion and recognise stress related conditions as having the potential for disrupting efficiency and productivity. Managing health should be recognised as a "line management" accountability. Managers should manage people as well as tasks, assets and projects. Obviously close liaison with the occupational health and personnel functions is likely to be required. Any problem can best be handled if it is possible to measure the extent of the situation or the number of people affected. In other words, **if you want to "manage" them being able to "measure" is essential.** Dealing with problems which individuals encounter must be handled with sensitivity. Confidentiality must be protected. There will be occasions where the manager is unaware of the difficulties being experienced by specific individuals but senior managers must understand the overall picture. Self-awareness and self-management must be promoted - the individual should be encouraged to learn skills and be aware of how he or she copes with increasing demands placed on them.

6.   The ICI/Zeneca Approach

HISTORY:- In the mid-1980s, the number of cases of stress related illness in ICI Pharmaceuticals reported to the Occupational Health Department indicated a disturbing upward trend. It may be of interest to display **THREE CASE HISTORIES** which demonstrate how stress related problems can be manifested.

Mr A has to co-ordinate the submission of the information to obtain a produce licence for a new compound. He works night and day - co-ordinating the efforts of people from individual departments. He has been told - "the business depends on you". His free time shrinks, his wife and family get the rough edge of his tongue over many months, he feels unsupported at work and unable to say he can't cope. At 9 p.m. after a train journey from London he bursts into tears on the station platform. Six months later he still lacks confidence but is learning to work more effectively and still find time for himself and his family.

Mrs B is engaged in a number of negotiations with other companies. New projects and negotiations are initiated regularly and require concentration over long hours. The projects require managing - she plays a key role in supporting and advancing each one. Works starts at 8 a.m. and never seems to stop. Holidays and weekends don't exist. Hobbies are a thing of the past. She wishes manpower requirements to manage new projects were planned at the outset. On two occasions she has been seen leaving her office at 7 p.m. Eventually she is taken off her job for two weeks rest. Mrs B is lucky - her overwork was recognised as such and she is not considered to have failed. Others are branded as 'weak'.

Mr C is promoted to senior staff level. He is well trained and capable. He works hard but is unable to prioritise his tasks and give each one full attention. No one asks him to outline his workload and allocate appropriate time to each task. He works 10 or 11 hours daily and is usually busy with work at weekends. The initial enthusiasm at the promotion is replaced by anxiety. He feels desperate, panic stricken and becomes depressed. One month's intensive treatment as an outpatient restores his health, vigour and enthusiasm. He needs training in managing his time. His manager needs to not only delegate the authority to look after various aspects of the departmental workload but share some of the responsibility for completion - within appropriate timescales.

Senior members of the occupational health and personnel functions met in late 1987 and a paper was drafted for presentation to the Chairman and Board of Directors of the Business. Within that paper, the likely reasons for the increase in the number of stress cases within the Pharmaceuticals business were highlighted. The list is probably applicable to many other organizations: (1) rapid growth; (2) increasing complexity; (3) organizational change to meet growth; (4) drive to become truly "international"; (5) pressure to sustain a high level of profit; (6) pressure to bring new products to the market; (7) tight control of manpower; (8) sheer volume of new work; (9) high quality of work expected; (10) commitment reaching a level where guilt is felt whenever work is not being done; (11) difficulty in matching people to jobs; (12) the volume of paper.

It was acknowledged that many of the people who get on the more senior jobs are relatively tough and resilient. For that reason, they may find it hard to understand why some of their subordinates find difficulty in coping. Stress may, however, affect individuals at all levels. The Board was asked, using the management system, to acknowledge the legitimacy of the concern and the proposals they were supporting to respond to it. The Board committed itself to a number of specific actions:

1. Staff to ensure that they dealt with essential tasks and were selective in use of time

2. A number of existing training activities to continue, e.g. "Time Management" and "Management of Change" courses

3. A one-day workshop to be established on the topic of stress

4. Guidance to be given on travel schedules, planning meetings etc.

5. Medical screening to include assessment of mental health - and guidance to be given to those requiring assistance

6. The match between people and jobs to be a priority. The personnel function to support this by continuing to improve selection and assessment techniques

7. The annual appraisal mechanism to be used to review workload and draft individual development plans, such that staff are given the opportunity to develop skills and acquire knowledge to match the demands of the job

8. Managers to manage **people** as well as projects. They are in the ideal situation to help and support their staff. As individuals may, however, choose to seek the assistance of a counsellor outside their normal sphere, the Personnel and Occupational Health functions should have sufficient trained people to meet this need. These counsellors must know when it is essential to refer individuals for more skilled or specialist support

The Strategy

Having determined the problems and possible solutions, the following set of aims was developed for a comprehensive stress management strategy. A working group was set up to find ways to implement these aims, comprising representatives from Occupational Health, personnel and external advisors. The brief was to create a comprehensive approach to preventing, recognising and treating mental health problems of all levels of severity. The following model appeared early in the discussions, and has proved a durable and self-explanatory schema.

Table 2.8

STRESS MANAGEMENT STRATEGY		
Levels	**Aims**	**Facilitators**
1.	Treat casualties	Occupational Health Professionals
2.	Detect other cases	Occupational Health Professionals/Managers
3.	Legitimise stress	Senior Management
4.	Increase awareness	Managers Training Occupational Health
5.	Teach skills	Training Occupational Health
6.	Improve Culture	Total Organization

This model consists of 6 levels. Most organizations fail to provide more than the 1st level of response i.e. the Physician and/or Nurse recognising casualties and dealing with them appropriately. This is a reactive response when presented with an anxious or distressed member of staff. Level 2 occurs when a more proactive approach is taken and early detection ensues thus minimising morbidity. At stage 3, as has occurred in Zeneca Pharmaceuticals, the topic becomes a subject for legitimate discussion i.e. stress related conditions are seen as having the potential for disrupting efficiency and productivity.

If the most senior managers are able to accept the need for further action (level 4), increasing awareness of mental health and the need to maintain it, can drive a number of initiatives - one of which, level 5, is to ensure that skills in management of self and others is integrated into the Company training programmes. Level 6 is the stage where the culture can begin to change on the benefit of individuals and the business performance itself. The existing organizational management culture had been essentially a type A, machismo-orientated approach to work where stress problems were usually concealed, and a complex mythology declared, for example, that a good manager is able to work effectively immediately after returning from a long haul flight. A magical belief that increasing seniority should bring immunity from stress maintained these attitudes.

Paradoxically, the organization was caring and supportive towards casualties, perhaps not least because of identification. Those who had required treatment for depression and anxiety usually received exemplary support, but this polarisation between those who had been affected by stress and a putative majority who had not, was in itself a stressor. The belief engendered by some stress management consultants, and in particular training consultancies, that the effective teaching of stress management skills abolishes endogenous depression, anxiety, chemical dependence or normal adjustment reactions, leads to fragmented approaches to stress management without effective safety nets for those who require treatment.

For all of these reasons, it seemed essential as a first step that the subject should be legitimised, that senior management approval and participation should be sought from the outset, and that a continuation, or increase, in referrals for treatment should not be seen as a failure. For these reasons the presentation to the Chairman and Board the Director and the initiative which was started a "top down" approach, instituted from the beginning to communicate these key points.

THE CHIEF EXECUTIVE OFFICER'S LETTER - If stress management is to be effective, it must percolate into the informal culture of the organization rather than just occupy the agenda of a few training sessions and then be forgotten. A pivotal step was the distribution to all departmental heads of a letter signed by the CEO. This reads as follows:

"I know that in recent months a number of Managers and employees have been concerned about the increasing demands of the business on employees and have seen this exemplified in a small but significant number of employees with serious problems.

The business will continue to expand and it is important that appropriate pressure is placed on staff. Some stress is good for both individuals and the business leading to job satisfaction, motivation and good performance. Too much or inappropriate pressure on people who are unable to cope with it is bad for them and bad for the business.

It is important for Managers to keep under surveillance the total workload on individuals and groups making sure that priorities and reasonable timescales are set. For example, I see it as important that staff have enough free time for outside pursuits. If work takes up more than a reasonable proportion of an individual's time, over too long a period, the business is unlikely to benefit in the long term. In this context an individual's holiday arrangements should only rarely be disrupted. The sensible planning and allocation of work within your department is a vital factor in maximising efficiency. I would ask you to pay particular attention to staff whose duties oblige them to do a lot of travelling, and ensure that they plan their schedules in a sensible way.

I have asked the Personnel and Occupational Health departments to pursue with you a number of detailed proposals designed to ensure a fuller appreciation of these issues and to minimise the incidence of stress related problems in this organization".

The letter led to a great deal of "behind the scenes" discussion and support; not surprisingly some senior managers were threatened by the idea of employees apparently being told to work less hard and to consider their family and social lives as a high priority. In some quarters there was genuine fear that the commercial momentum of the organization might be impaired. It will come as no surprise to those involved in organizational development work that this was not the case and indeed it seems likely that the reverse effect occurred. There is every indication that commitment and efficiency have improved. There is no doubt, however, that this letter and the known existence of high level working parties, increased interest and underlined credibility to all staff.

Stress Management Workshops - agreement was reached that four pilot stress management workshops would be held. The objectives for the workshops were set as follows:

1. To raise awareness of what is meant by "Stress"
2. To legitimise Stress as a subject for discussion in the Business
3. To show a range of Stress Management skills with a view to further skills training
4. To practice two key Stress Management skills, i.e. listening and relaxing

The organization and presentation of these workshops was a joint responsibility shared by the Training Section of Personnel and the Occupational Health Departments. The fact that this was the first such collaboration, and the knowledge that the participants for the first two workshops would include the Chairman and Board of Directors were in themselves stressors and the pre-workshop discussions were nervous and tentative, with considerable difficulty in agreeing the precise structure and content. It seems a universal paradox that stress management projects cause considerable stress for those designing and implementing them, perhaps partly because of the dynamics of allowing oneself to be seen as an "expert" on stress who should, therefore, have no problems in dealing with it oneself. The open rejection of this myth at the beginning of every workshop relieves the tension for all involved.

A rudimentary attempt was made to evaluate the effectiveness of these workshops by simple feedback questionnaires.

Pilot Stress Management Workshops
They were attended by 85% of all Directors, General Managers and Heads of Department. Feedback questionnaires found that 66% were in favour of the event as run, 18% were broadly in favour and 16% were critical.

As a result of this initially encouraging feedback the Workshops have been continued, and have evolved into a well rehearsed event which is subjected to continual audit and development. The workshops started in January 1988 and by the beginning of 1993 almost 700 individuals had attended. It was a deliberate policy to start at the top and work outwards - the first three workshops were attended by most of the Directors of the business.

The workshops began as a synthesis of information and skills training techniques drawn from management training and from the treatment of patients with stress problems. It became clear that the workshop model was an appropriate one, with group tasks and the sharing of experiences playing a vital part. Consideration of case studies, often only slightly modified from real life stories, provided a useful vehicle: These were originally presented on paper, then by role play using a professional actor, and then by the production of two high quality videos depicting fictional case histories, which offer the benefits of reproducibility, dramatic interest, and realistic portrayal of a variety of familiar situations.

The idea behind the stress management workshop is relatively straightforward. It is to show people that stress is a normal part of a healthy life which can, however, get out of control. It is important therefore to be able to recognise - in oneself and others - when stress levels are becoming too great, and to do something about it before "overload" is reached; that is, to learn "stress management" skills. **The workshop is not intended to be a counselling forum for people who are deemed to have stress related problems**. The workshop is spread over 1 full day with a further half-day event one month later. The organizers point out that participation in any workshop activity is voluntary and that all discussions are strictly confidential. As with most successful training programmes, the workshop involves a great deal of active participation. The day is relaxed and informal. The first exercise is simple and deceptively effective. Privately and in pairs, each participant spends 5 minutes telling their partner the sources of stress in their lives. One person talks and the other listens. Roles are then reversed. Back at base, everyone is asked in turn to describe what if any value such an exercise had but not to reveal the details. What emerges is surprisingly uniform; that there is a large degree of empathy - what stresses one person more often than not also stresses the other; and that simply to have someone who is patiently listening to you, and showing genuine interest in what you are saying, is in itself of immense value. Already, one hour into the day one of the big barriers to success for stress management is crumbling. Stress is not confined to one or two individuals, and is a legitimate subject for discussion. A group "brainstorming" session on the general topic of "what stresses me" enables the course participants to focus more closely on those everyday strains which produce the symptoms of stress. Late trains, cantankerous teenage children, prevaricating estate agents.

A specially commissioned video chronicles the events leading up to the nervous breakdown of John, a (fictitious) "hard-pressed" ICI/ZENECA Pharmaceuticals employee. In the ensuing discussion the events depicted are picked over with a fine-toothed comb. Why did he take on more work than he could handle? What was the responsibility of his boss? Could the signs have been spotted earlier? A second video shows how a different fictitious employee "gets it right", and avoids the consequences of his unfortunate colleague. Finally, a brief introduction is given to various techniques of relaxation.

The Workshops Focus on the 4 Key Areas Where the Effects of Stress Can Be Seen
This is best captured by reference to the following stress cycle model.(Figure 2.26)

A. THE DISTRESS CYCLE

(i) Behavioural Changes
Stress affects eating, drinking and smoking patterns and can make people restless and unable to settle. Some of us "comfort eat" by nibbling at sweet and savory snacks and then feeling guilty about it afterwards. Other people lose their appetite and become hungry and irritable. Alcohol is a very effective stress reducer, and is used on social occasions for precisely this reason. Our studies have shown that people smoke more and drink more when they are tense.

(ii) Physiological Changes
The "fight or flight" responses are activated. This is very helpful at preparing the body to produce high physical output over the short-term and in doing so we "burn off" the adrenaline. If carried on over a long period of time it can produce indigestion, fatigue and heart problems.

(iii) Emotional Changes
When stressed we feel irritable, anxious and restless - the sort of experience that most people have had before an exam an interview or a difficult meeting. Normally these feelings pass when we are distracted by the task in hand. If the stressors are less obvious, the feelings may become more permanent, making it difficult for the individual to sleep properly and to start the next day feeling refreshed and ready for action.

(iv)   Cognitive Changes

"Cognitive" means to do with thinking functions. Stress can reduce concentration, make us feel that our memory is not working properly and reduce our capacity to take on the jobs we feel under pressure to complete.

Any combination of these effects increase the stress load experienced by individuals and can create a vicious cycle.

Distress Cycle

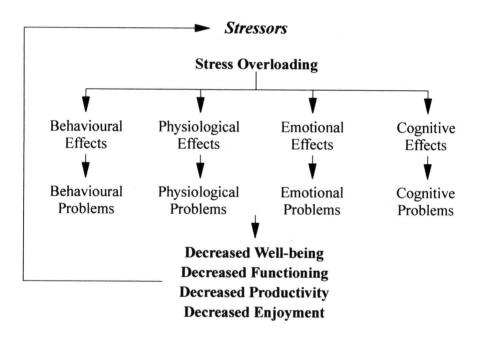

Figure 2.26

B.   THE WELLNESS CYCLE

This diagram (Figure 2.27) introduced the concept of individuals developing skills to help them monitor feelings and behaviour in each of the four areas.   If they can respond to stress by activating effective coping resources, then they can deal with the demands more effectively, thereby reducing their overall stress load.

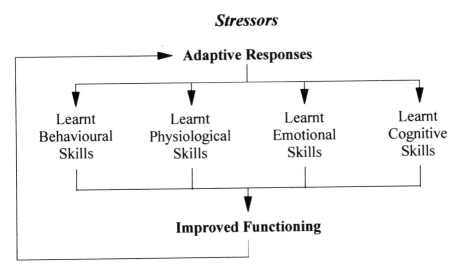

Wellness Cycle

Stressors

(COGNITIVE means to do with the THINKING FUNCTIONS)

Figure 2.27

The workshops present the theoretical basis for our behaviour patterns. They emphasise the benefits of the practical development of specific skills. The skills are based on the application of the wellness cycle to everyday life.

Impact of Intervention

Do the Workshops Produce Measurable Benefits?

Three separate approaches have been used:

1. **Validation Using Questionnaires**

It was decided in 1989 to ask participants to complete questionnaires **BEFORE** attending the workshop and again **THREE MONTHS LATER**. Shortly after this component was added, a second half-day was arranged as a review point at this time.

Questionnaires for this purpose had to meet the following criteria:

1. They had to be concise enough to be completed in a total of less than 30 minutes
2. Validated for test/retest reliability, and
3. Normative data had to be available

As we wished to quantify stress, suitable questionnaires were the Occupational Stress Indicator (OSI) and the General Health Questionnaire (GHQ) in its 12, 28 and 30 item variants. The GHQ-30 was chosen. It must be emphasised that this is not a controlled study. Questionnaire data has been collected on more than 700 employees over more than four years, however, and the results are strikingly consistent.

Stress levels within the organization are high normal (mean GHQ 25.2), with a consistently increasing trend. The average pre-workshop score has increased by 15% over four years, with noticeable increases at times of organizational stress such as the takeover threat in 1991. The distribution of scores shows a "bulge" caused by the high scores of the subgroup who are experiencing high levels of stress at any given moment: their scores are strikingly high on occasion, and it is a chastening thought that some individuals in the workplace are admitting to more stress than patients being admitted to a psychiatric clinic. It seems unlikely that their work performance will be unaffected.

When retested between two and three months later, mean GHQ scores have fallen by 15-20%, and this improvement is demonstrated in those with normal, high or very high pre-workshop scores. This latter observation is very important, since an effective intervention needs to reach the target group rather than simply preaching to the converted.

2. Number of Cases Presenting

Figure 2.28 displays the overall number of individuals within the organization who needed to be referred to psychiatrists or psychologists or who attended the ICI/ZENECA Health Centres or their own family doctor's clinics over the last 10 years.

No. of Referrals

Figure 2.28: Referrals to Psychiatrists/Counselling/Attendance at Zeneca Pharmaceuticals Health Centres (UK Sites)

We can reasonably assume that this results from improved **earlier intervention** as average GHQ scores from the workshops held in recent years indicate increasing subjective stress levels.

3. Feedback

Comments from individuals attending workshops continues to be positive. Individuals report a much greater awareness of the demands placed on them and how they can best organize their work, domestic and social lives to increase efficiency and enjoyment. Demands for places on the workshop remains high and the training is seen as part of essential management training. The workshops have also helped to identify wider training needs such as the development of improved skills in Assertiveness, Time Management etc. The 'Getting It Right' Stress Management training package has been formatted for ease of use throughout ICI and ZENECA. It has been welcomed by many other organizations, institutions, Health Authorities and Health Care providers, not only in the UK but internationally.

There is clear evidence from the data available, all of which supports our observations that:
1. Stress levels within the organization are high
2. Some individuals are adversely affected by stress
3. The interventions described above, especially the Stress Management Workshops, are effective in improving symptoms and restoring function quickly

The project continues, and a current objective is to refine and extend the assessments, preferably by including a control group.

Analysis of Benefit

Traditionally much of the justification for stress management training has been based on increased subjective well-being. However, since the mid-1980's, a growing body of research has demonstrated objective improvement in cardio-vascular health resulting from behaviour modification, including relaxation training, as a first-line treatment for hypertension in general practice and in improving outcome for post-myocardial infarct patients. (Friedman et al., American Heart Journal 1986; Lifestyle Heart Trial 1990; Patel & Marmot 1988, etc.). There is also a need to evaluate cost benefit in terms of employee productivity, employee turnover and sickness and absence rates. This, however, is notoriously difficult to do with any accuracy because of the number of complicating factors which prevent the assumption of a fixed base line.

Although the development of the project was empirical, its key aims are supported by the draft proposals established by the US National Institute of Occupational Safety and Health in 1986 which were:

1. Attention to job design
2. Improved surveillance
3. Improved training, transfer of information and resource development
4. An enriched mental health component within industry (occupational) health services

The ICI/ZENECA Pharmaceuticals Strategy was carefully thought out and based on the following elements:

1. Early involvement of Directors and General Managers
2. Collaboration between Occupational Health, Training, Organizational experts and managers
3. Effective communication with managers regarding the importance of Mental Health and Stress
4. The adoption of suitable parameters to quantify the business position
5. The introduction of well planned, professional training and educational programmes, including finely tuned, validated skills training workshops - based around 2 high quality videos
6. Effective publicity with the production of leaflets, booklets and other educational training aids
7. A complementary counselling and treatment service
8. Monitoring, using appropriate measures, to assess the benefits of the above initiatives
9. The implementation of a cultural change initiative within the Business leading to better development of individuals and targeting of organizational efforts to agreed goals

ZENECA has a Safety, Health and Environment **Policy and Management System**, 19 **Standards** were issued which detail the measures which must be complied with by all managers and staff throughout the organization. There must be more 'detail' if these are to be converted into workable procedures to be used at all ZENECA locations. A Guideline on 'Stress' is being drafted during the course of 1995. This will address:

(i)   the benefits (to the organization and individual members of staff) of encouraging good (mental) health

(ii)   the activities/tasks/projects likely to generate work-related stress

(iii)   the assessment of the capability and competencies of staff at recruitment and at significant changes of job demand to ensure that job requirements are matched to employees throughout their career with ZENECA

(iv)   the provision of training for Managers and staff to recognise stress in themselves and others and to identify the skills required to manage it

(v)   the need to train managers to manage in a way which does not generate unnecessary stress in their team

(vi)   the provision of training/education for staff on how to lead a balanced life which is both productive and enjoyable

(vii)   the creation of an environment or structure that enables employees with stress related problems to seek help within their workplace

(viii) the provision of counselling services which can give help and advice

(ix)   the maintenance of links with external agencies in order to make more specialised support available

The well-being of employees and the success of an organization can go 'hand in hand'. The following model may be useful in this regard:

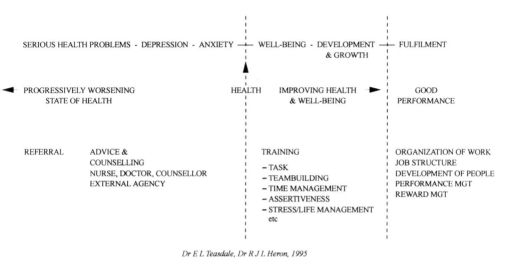

SERIOUS HEALTH PROBLEMS - DEPRESSION - ANXIETY — WELL-BEING - DEVELOPMENT — FULFILMENT
& GROWTH

PROGRESSIVELY WORSENING   HEALTH   IMPROVING HEALTH   GOOD
STATE OF HEALTH   & WELL-BEING   PERFORMANCE

REFERRAL   ADVICE &   TRAINING   ORGANIZATION OF WORK
            COUNSELLING   JOB STRUCTURE
            NURSE, DOCTOR, COUNSELLOR   – TASK   DEVELOPMENT OF PEOPLE
            EXTERNAL AGENCY   – TEAMBUILDING   PERFORMANCE MGT
                                        – TIME MANAGEMENT   REWARD MGT
                                        – ASSERTIVENESS
                                        – STRESS/LIFE MANAGEMENT
                                        etc

Dr E L Teasdale, Dr R J L Heron, 1995

Figure 2.29 Individual Well-Being/Business Success

As will be seen, organization structuring and staff development and reward are key to both success and good health. Whilst 'Performance Management' (including the setting of 'targets') may focus individuals on priority issues - the process itself may cause stress to many. The organization of work should be supported by training initiatives to provide skills and information. However, some individuals (probably **most** over time) will require advice and support. A complementary counselling/EAP programme will be required.

Summary

Defining objectives and accountability clearly, setting priorities and managing time effectively is essential. In an innovative and demanding environment, maintaining the health of staff and managing stress positively is likely to improve productivity, reduce errors, increase creativity, improve decision-making and lead to enhanced job satisfaction.

A policy for Health with clear Guidelines for Managers is essential. This should not be a stand alone initiative but a part of an integrated approach to managing a high quality organization. The challenge in any organization, is to allow and encourage an appropriate amount of stress or pressure, to enhance the performance of individuals, the departments where they work and thus the Business and Organization as a whole.

Chapter 3
The Organizational and Economic Costs of Stress:
A Measurement Perspective

Aside from the impact that stress may have "on the bottom line", European organizations have increasing obligations to assess the health and safety of employees. Although the recent European framework directive on health and safety at work (89/391/EEC) contains no specific reference to stress and well being at work, a certain amount of attention is given to these aspects in Article 6 of the directive (Kompier et. al., 1994). As with any other item of organizational expenditure, investment in stress prevention and health promotion activities also has to be supported and justified by a sound and convincing business case if it is to mobilize commitment.. Interventions, particularly those which involve major changes in organizational structure and working practices, like the ABB initiative, are potentially disruptive to business and require long term investment and commitment. As the ABB case demonstrates, it is good practice to first conduct a small scale pilot intervention. Causal relationships between interventions and benefits need to be established, as far as possible. This means that critical success factors, key processes and performance indicators have to be clearly defined from the outset. An organization needs to know its starting point in order to assess the benefits derived. As the case studies illustrate, interventions can produce both qualitative and quantitative benefits and achieve favourable returns on its investment.

Corporate Costs

As a starting point, O'Donnell (1984) suggests the potential corporate benefits of stress prevention and health promotion activities can be considered to lie in four main areas:- productivity improvements, reduced employee health and insurance costs, reduced human resource development costs and organizational image. There are also other areas and indices which could be taken into consideration, e.g. product quality.

PRODUCTIVITY IMPROVEMENTS - These are likely to occur as a result of:-

- **Reduced absenteeism** - this may be the outcome of a decrease in the incidence of sick leave or a decrease in the duration of sick leave. As a result, there is likely to be less disruption and more potential flexibility in work planning schedules.

- **Improved morale and willingness to co-operate** and to accommodate change - Senior management at ABB consider that a major benefit of their programme has been a positive acceptance by their workforce of the need for continuous change (Nilson, 1995)

- **Lowered operating costs** - employees with a more positive attitude towards their employer and their work are less likely to misuse organizational resources

- **Improved ability to perform** -a healthy workforce is a productive workforce

- **Higher quality workforce** - as illustrated by the ABB experience, stress intervention programmes can reduce staff turnover rates. The presence of such programmes can also change the corporate culture and so improve the organization's ability to attract new high quality employees

REDUCTIONS IN EMPLOYEE HEALTH AND RELATED COSTS - These are likely to occur as a result of:

- **A decrease in the direct costs of sickness and absence** - currently met by the organization e.g. sick pay provisions, employer contributions to private healthcare funds. It is recognised that within a European context that the magnitude of these savings will vary depending upon local arrangements.

- **An improvement in accident and safety records** - which if experience based, will result in a reduction in liability and accident insurance premiums

- **A reduction in the time and administrative costs** involved in processing employee claims and benefits

REDUCED HUMAN RESOURCE DEVELOPMENT COSTS - These are likely to occur because fewer demands will be placed on the budgetary resources for

- **Recruitment**
- **Education and Training.**

THE ORGANIZATIONAL IMAGE - Positive benefits are likely to accrue as the organization will be perceived both internally and externally as a

- **Concerned and responsible employer**

    Both the ABB and Zeneca programmes have received considerable publicity. The ABB and Zeneca training videos have been used by other organizations.

Obviously, it is also important to consider the potential costs associated with stress prevention and health promotion activities. These can be considered as falling into four main areas:- organizational costs, administrative costs, intervention costs and participant costs.

ORGANIZATIONAL COSTS which include:

- **Impact on the organizational culture and the attitudes of its members**
- **Impact on the daily work routine** - lost production costs as a result of employee attendance at training events etc.
- **Opportunity cost** - the loss of potential benefits that might be derived from some other use of the resources
- **Long term commitment** and the possible negative effects on employee morale and expectations if an intervention was subsequently discontinued or reversed.

ADMINISTRATIVE COSTS - As the case studies illustrate, the support of senior management is critical to an intervention which has a cost implication. Interventions invariably also require considerable planning and liaison with different functions, departmental heads, staff representatives and external agencies.

THE COST OF THE INTERVENTION ITSELF in terms of its:-

- **Development, Design and Promotional costs**
- **Implementation costs**

■   **Operational costs**

PARTICIPANT COSTS - The introduction of an intervention may highlight psychological problems or existing health conditions which need to be addressed and may have cost implications. Change in itself may be stressful for some employees. Although this was not specifically mentioned in the case studies, it is difficult to envisage that the kinds of intervention introduced at ABB and Nelissen Van Egteren Bouw Heerlen BV did not meet with some managerial resistance as potentially threatening and eroding their own responsibilities and power base.

Economic Costs

Both the Swedish and Dutch case studies demonstrate the methods used to conduct a cost-benefit analysis from a corporate perspective. However, the economic consequences of stress can be measured and analysed from different perspectives which have implications at State and Community level.

Stress and its economic consequences, in different perspectives

In order to be able to measure and analyse the economic consequences of stress and stress programmes, it is important to determine the measurement perspective. Depending on what perspective is used to measure the consequences of the stress programme, the result can vary. It is not only the choice of perspective that separates the economic outcomes; methods of measurement and the economic consequences also vary. What is measured as a cost at the level of public administration need not mean costs at the level of private enterprise. In the same way, employees' loss of welfare does not imply costs for the company.

Three Cost Units

There are also situations in which the cost units - society, the company and the individual - wind up in a borderline zone, where the costs of stress are borne by all three. It is important to look at perhaps these situations in particular in order to identify arguments for taking measures that reduce the negative consequences of stress. (It is important to bring the matter to the attention of politicians/policymakers. Improvements in public finances rarely motivate private companies to adopt stress programmes. What the companies can get for the money ey invest must be clearly stated. Everyone has to gain something!)

n example of such a situation is stress that causes illnesses that in turn results in the
nployee having to go on early retirement pension. The costs are borne by the government
the form of disability pension, by the company in the form of loss of knowledgeable and
perienced manpower, as well as by the disabled person in the form of the loss of welfare
at early retirement often means. A methodology for the establishment of the economic costs
stress at national level is outlined in another publication by the Foundation entitled "Socio-
onomic costs of work stress in two EU Member States" (Levi & Lunde-Jensen, 1996)

he economic consequences of a stress programme can be summarised in figure 3.1. The
gure also indicates the most common methods of financially evaluating the different areas.

Calculating and Unit Costs
3 perspectives

- **National**
Socioeconomic costs and benefits

- **Organisational**
Financial costs and benefits

- **Individual**
Loss of welfare

igure 3.1

Perspective Determines Method of Measurement

At the public administration level, it is common to use theories of economics derived from methods of calculation that show the consequences in terms of public finances of stress and stress programmes. Reduction in national welfare are studied using socioeconomic analyses. The employee bears a portion of the economic consequences caused by stress. These consequences are usually subsumed under the rubric, loss of welfare. Examples of such loss of welfare are, e.g. loss of work or the opportunity to pursue a profession or trade, lost opportunities for further education, sickness and involuntary early retirement caused by stress, absence from work, anxiety about one's future and one's job etc.

When the economic consequences of stress programmes are being studied, the measurement and analysis of the effects must be carried out in all three areas. The consequences of stress for public finances, private companies finances and the individual's own personal finances, are not isolated events, but rather affect and are affected by each other. Each area of measurement has its own measurement tools.

Cause-and-Effect is the Basis for the Economic Measurements

The use of the calculation methods always presupposes that the cause-and-effect relationship is established and that the measures taken to reduce stress actually have caused the costs or benefits in focus for the economic calculation. This is often difficult to establish because most interventions are multi-faceted in their approach and therefore it is often difficult to isolate the effectiveness of individual components. Many studies which have assessed the efficacy of interventions are also methodologically weakened by the absence of control groups (Cooper & Cartwright, 1994). If these important connections are lacking, the results from the case studies cannot be used as proof of the positive economic effects of the stress programme. In the case study of the construction company, an attempt is made to establish cause-and-effect using a regression analysis that shows how sick leave has been affected by the leadership programme. The evidence from this case study is also strengthened by the existence of control groups.

A Complex Problem Requires Many Methods of Measurement

When the cause-and-effect relationship between the stress programme and the economic and organizational consequences is vague, complex and spread over a large area, the financial consequences of stress for the company can be studied through direct and indirect measurements. Examples of indirect measurements are measurement of work time, absence, sick leave, external or internal staff turnover, the extent and effects of training and staff development initiatives etc.

Individual measurements alone, e.g. sick leave, are not sufficient to explain the complex situations in which stress programmes are implemented. Therefore it is important to have many indicators from different areas, in order to make possible analyses based on a comprehensive view of the economic and organizational consequences.

It is also important to develop methods of measurement, for the analysis of the economic consequences of stress, that make it possible to learn by doing. It is an old truth that problems that can be understood can also be solved.

Measurement of Costs and Benefits of Stress Programmes

Stress has financial consequences for companies, both in the short and the long term. Some of the consequences can be measured directly, others indirectly. Some of the consequences can always be measured using quantitative methods, e.g. personnel costs, while others always require qualitative measurement, e.g. the organization's capacity or health.

Financial Measurements

Companies are constantly measuring their rationality by using financial and operative measures of rationality. The financial measures of rationality are liquidity, solvency, profitability etc. These measures can be indirectly affected by the consequences of the stress programme. An example from the case studies shows how co-operation within the company improved. Shorter throughput times, processing times, etc., can lead to less capital being tied up in production and a more effective use of the financial resources of the company.

Operative Measures

The operative measures of the rationality of a company, i.e. productivity, quality and effectiveness, are, on the other hand, often directly affected by the effects of the stress programme. Here, the ABB study is a good example of how the operative measures, e.g. throughput time and level of service, are affected. It was however, not the stress programme alone that lead to these results, but rather the total investment in the "industrial revolution", or, the T-50 programme which led to macro-level changes in the organizational culture.

Basic Data for Measurement Lacking

Extensive research has been done on the consequences of stress for the individual and the organization. However, the financial consequences for the company have not been studied to the same degree. In the literature, measurement areas are presented, but the empirical studies that could show the practical applications of measurement are almost completely absent. Since the fundamental problem - how the financial consequences of stress for private and public companies are quantified and analysed in the company's financial routines - has not been solved, there is no basic data available that could guide the measurement of the financial consequences of the stress programmes for the companies, either.

The problem is thus not the lack of economic calculation methods, but the lack of factual material on which to base calculations. Instead of focusing interest on individual cost-benefit analyses, it would be better to investigate where and how to obtain the basic data for the calculations. Another resulting problem is the verifiability of the variables in the companies' financial systems. It should be possible to answer questions such as the one described in the case studies - of whether the cost of sick leave is verifiable or simply a taxed cost.

In these case studies, a first attempt to quantify the economic consequences of stress has been made. The result might have been different if the accountants had been able to follow the consequences of the stress programmes right from the start. After the programme has been carried out, it is just about impossible to reconstruct the procedure. Further studies of an inter-disciplinary character are needed.

The consequences of stress for the individual and the organization are well known in the literature of behavioural science and stress research. The consequences of stress must also be made quantifiable in companies' financial, production and personnel statistics.

Problems of measurement technique in evaluating the economic consequences of the stress programmes

Accounting Conventions Steer

Business economics, like all other sciences, has its paradigms that organize theories, measurement methods, models and the language of accounting. The theories that steer accounting are commonly referred to as the accounting conventions and are generally accepted in the field of business economics. The accounting conventions are international. This international system of rules is presented in summary in "Framework for the Preparation and Presentation of Financial Statements" put out by the International Accounting Committee. The conventions include some twenty recommendations, which are presented in condensed form in figure 3.2.

Accounting Conventions

Conventions

1. Understandability

2. Relevance

3. Reliability
   - Neutrality
   - Prudence
   - Completeness

4. Comparability

Satisfied by case study

5. Constraints on relevant and reliable information

6. Timeliness

7. Balance between benefit and cost

8. Balance between qualitative characteristics

9. True and fair view/fair presentation

Figure 3.2

An examination of all three case studies shows that none of them satisfies the requirements of the accounting conventions. The difficulties of measuring the economic consequences of the stress programmes appear when the statistical material is to be verified, in the difficulty of finding a balance between costs and benefits as well as in use of quantitative and qualitative measures. In the pharmaceuticals company, the economical consequences of stress are presented summarily, but a number of examples of qualitative consequences are described in words. In the case studies from the industrial company and the construction companies, both quantitative and qualitative measures are presented. This, however, without their having been verified.

A Larger Measurement Problem

These measurement problems reveal yet a larger problem, resulting from the lack of relevant accounting of the companies' personnel costs. The companies present their personnel costs as one single item - wage costs - in their statement of accounts. However, the extent to which the wage costs are a representation of the total personnel costs is not always made clear. Nor what the wage costs consists of. How large a portion of the wage costs is costs for workers' attendance (time worked) and how much for their absence (sick leave and other absenteeism) is not indicated either. Nor is it made clear how large a portion of the wage costs has been used for training, internal and external mobility, rehabilitation of those on long-term sick leave, etc.

What does business accounting actually measure?

Another problem that the case-studies reveal is the organization of the accounting systems. The accounting is often geared more towards measuring the capacity of machines, and the use of materials, technique and capital, than towards describing the development of personnel costs. Consequently, the focus is on the place where the cost first arose, instead of on the event that caused the cost. Events that affect the development of the different components of wage costs are not presented even though the information is available in the company's wage records. Insufficient accounting and analysis of costs that taken together constitute the company's total personnel cost, makes the measurement and analysis of the economic consequences of the stress programme more difficult.

Table 3.1 : A Comparison of the Case Studies in Terms of Variables Considered

Case Study	Variables that describe the organization's capacity and work environment	Variables that describe personnel and production costs
Industrial Company ABB	* well-defined, motivation goals * flexibility * versatility * fair/motivating system of rewards * work enrichment * system of rotation * "Tool box" for staff development	* sick leave * other absenteeism * staff turnover * delivery reliability * throughput times * capital tied up in production and storage
Pharmaceuticals Company Zeneca	* training * improving health and well-being * good performance * organization of work * job structure * development of people * performance MCT * reward MCT * referrals to psychiatrists * counselling, attendance * stress management	* well-being * functioning * productivity * enjoyment * sick leave * staff turnover * absenteeism (mentioned but not measured)
Construction Company	* working conditions * job content * labour relations * health, behaviour * complaints about health and well-being * physical stress in the working situation * stress-related fatigue * management activity * educating employees in detecting stress-related complaints * higher motivation * high-quality performance * improved relations between co-workers and management * greater capacity to spot and solve problems * less failure through improved information	* termination of employment * number of accidents * number of days absent due to accidents * absenteeism * replacement costs

Simultaneous Accounting

The most common measures of a positive development in an organization's capacity are increased flexibility, high motivation and increased enjoyment of work. It is also important that these measures, which show how the organization's capacity and personnel costs have developed, are presented at the same time.

The Organization's Capacity or Health

The economic consequences of the stress programme can be measured in different ways, using different methods and from different perspectives. The measurements are often partial, as the case-studies have shown.

From Measuring Personnel Costs to Measuring the Organization's capacity (or health)

The difficulties associated with identifying the connections between the stress programme and its economic consequences also reveal other problems of measurement that result from the complexity of the situation measured. As the case studies show, no stress programme was carried out as an isolated investment by the companies. In the construction company, the stress programme was a part of a larger investment in leadership; in the industrial company, ABB, a part of the decade's "industrial revolution", and in the pharmaceuticals company, an investment in the employees' health and leadership.

In the complex situations where the stress programme is implemented, it is probably not sufficient to take individual variables as measures of the economic consequences of the stress programme. Instead, in the case studies, measurements have been taken over a broader area and could be described as measurement of the organization's capacity or health.

An investment in the company's competitiveness

By the organization's capacity is meant its competitiveness, i.e. activities that increase the company's strength on the market. Such activities are, e.g. investments in increased mobility, achieved through development projects, broad training of all employees. Activities such as rotation and work enrichment are parts of investments that can increase the organization's capacity. Increased advance planning is achieved through decentralization and projects to promote customer satisfaction often begin with an investment in the employees and their work environment.

The ABB study is a typical example of a broad investment in the organization's capacity that makes the company more flexible, increases advance planning and reinforces its renewal ability. Consequently, it is natural that the consequences of the stress programme cannot be found in studies of how sick leave - in itself a negative measure of effect - has developed, but rather in the consequences which show how the company's competitiveness has improved.

Issues of measurement may be complex but still need to be addressed and incorporated in the evaluation of any intervention strategy. Organizations may be reluctant to introduce or will abandon or lose interest in intervention programmes in the absence of a methodology by which to ascertain demonstrable benefits. As discussed, because it is difficult or perhaps impossible retrospectively, to entirely reconstruct pre-intervention data, baseline measures have to be decided upon and the appropriate data collected prior to the intervention. A lot of the statistical data will already exist in some shape or form within the organization and will only need to be centrally collated and integrated. Software packages are increasingly being developed which are of use in this area.

Because stress impacts upon individual and organizational functioning in diverse ways, the indices selected to assess the outcome of stress reduction strategies should similarly reflect this diversity. Ideally, a well designed evaluation mechanism should include a pre/post comparison of indices which relate to **productivity**, e.g. output, error count, throughput time etc., **personnel and staffing costs**, e.g. absenteeism, labour turnover, early retirement and **organizational capacity or health** e.g. job satisfaction, creativity etc. Whilst productivity indices and personnel costs can be numerically quantified and directly assessed against investment costs, **organizational health or capacity** is of a more qualitative nature. However, there are reliable and valid questionnaire instruments available which could be used to measure these outcomes.

Chapter 4
Organizational Stress Intervention Strategies:
Current Practices

Types and Levels of Intervention

Any organization which seeks to establish and maintain the best state of physical, mental and social well being of its employees needs to have policies and procedures which comprehensively address health and safety. These policies will include procedures to manage stress, based on the needs of the organizations and its members, and will be regularly reviewed and evaluated.

There are a number of options to consider in looking at the prevention of stress, which are termed **primary** (e.g. stressor reduction), **secondary** (e.g. stress management) and **tertiary** (e.g. Employee Assistance Programmes/Counselling) levels of prevention and address different stages in the stress process (Murphy, 1988).

Primary prevention is concerned with taking action to modify or eliminate sources of stress inherent in the work environment and so reduce their negative impact on the individual. The 'interactionist' approach to stress (Cox 1978; Edwards & Cooper 1990) depicts stress as the consequences of the "lack of fit" between the needs and demands of the individual and his/her environment. The focus of primary interventions is in adapting the environment to "fit" the individual.

Elkin & Rosch (1990) summarise a useful range of possible strategies to reduce workplace stressors:-

- Redesign the task
- Redesign the work environment
- Establish flexible work schedules
- Encourage participative management
- Include the employee in career development
- Analyse work roles and establish goals
- Provide social support and feedback

- Build cohesive teams
- Establish fair employment policies
- Share the rewards

A number of general recommendations for reducing job stress have been put forward by the US body, NIOSH in the National Strategy for the Prevention of Work Related Psychological Disorders (Sauter, Murphy & Hurrell, 1990). A few of these recommendations are listed below:

Work load and work pace. Demands (both physical and mental) should be commensurate with the capabilities and resources of workers, avoiding underload as well as overload. Provisions should be made to allow recovery from demanding tasks or for increased control by workers over characteristics such as work pace of demanding tasks.

Work schedule. Work schedules should be compatible with demands and responsibilities outside the job. Recent trends toward flexitime, a compressed work week, and job sharing are examples of positive steps in this direction. When schedules involve rotating shifts, the rate of rotation should be stable and predictable.

Job future. Ambiguity should be avoided in opportunities for promotion and career or skill development, and in matters pertaining to job security. Employees should be clearly informed of imminent organizational developments that may affect their employment.

Social environment. Jobs should provide opportunities for personal interaction, both for purposes of emotional support and for actual help as needed in accomplishing assigned tasks.

Job content. Job tasks should be designed to have meaning and provide stimulation, and an opportunity to use skills. Job rotation or increasing the scope (enlargement/enrichment) of work activities are ways to improve narrow, fragmented work activities that fail to meet these criteria.

Both the Dutch and Swedish case studies represent examples of primary intervention and are illustrative of organizational action to reduce workplace stressors. In the Dutch case, this involved changes in the communication and consultative processes. In the Swedish case, it involved quite dramatic changes in the methods and style of work organization. Indirectly, such strategies are often a vehicle for culture change. Obviously, as the type of action required by an organization will vary according to the kinds of stressors operating, any intervention needs to be guided by some prior diagnosis or stress audit to identify the organizational, site or departmental specific stressors which are responsible for employee stress. Again, this approach was illustrated in the Dutch case study where interviews and questionnaires were used to establish the kinds of stressors which were associated with stress related fatigue and burnout.

Secondary Prevention is essentially concerned with the prompt detection and management of experienced stress by increasing awareness and improving the stress management skills of the individual through training and educative activities. Individual factors can alter or modify the way employees exposed to workplace stressors perceive and react to this environment. Each individual has their own personal stress threshold which is why some people thrive in a certain setting and others suffer. As discussed (Chapter 1) this threshold will vary between individuals and across different situations and life stages. Some key factors or "moderator" variables which influence on individual's vulnerability to stress include:

* their personality
* their coping strategies
* age
* gender
* attitudes
* training
* past experiences
* the degree of social support which is available from family, friends and work colleagues

The UK case study is an example of secondary prevention which focused on developing self awareness and initially providing individuals with a number of basic relaxation techniques.

The workshops also identified other areas of skills training which were subsequently addressed. Secondary level intervention also formed part of the integrated approach adopted by the Dutch construction company. Although the scale of the training was less extensive and appears to have been confined to managerial groups. Health promotion activities and lifestyle modification programmes also fall into the category of secondary level interventions.

Stress education and stress management training serve a useful function in helping individuals to recognise the symptoms of stress, and to overcome much of the negativity and stigma still associated with the stress label. Awareness activities and skills training programmes designed to improve relaxation techniques, cognitive coping skills and work/lifestyle modification skills (e.g. time management courses or assertiveness training) have an important part to play in extending the individual's physical and psychological resources. They are particularly useful in helping individuals deal with stressors inherent in the work environment that cannot be changed and have to be "lived with", like, for example, job insecurity. Such training can also prove helpful to individuals in dealing with stress in other aspects of their life, i.e. non-work related. However, the role of secondary prevention is essentially one of *damage limitation*, often addressing the **consequences** rather than the **sources** of stress which may be inherent in the organization's structure or culture. They are concerned with improving the 'adaptability' of the individual to the environment. Consequently, this type of intervention is often described as "the band aid" or inoculation approach. Because it is implicitly assumed that the organization will not change but continue to be stressful, therefore, the individual has to develop and strengthen his/her resistance to that stress. The continued demand for the stress management programme and the increasing stress levels reported by Dr Eric Teasdale at Zeneca are perhaps indicative of the organization's acceptance that stress is an inherent and enduring feature of the working environment which has to be "coped and lived with".

Tertiary Prevention is concerned with the treatment, rehabilitation and recovery process of those individuals who have suffered or are suffering from serious ill health as a result of stress. Interventions at the tertiary level typically involve the provision of counselling services for employee problems in the work or personal domain. Such services are either provided by in-house counsellors or outside agencies in the form of an Employee Assistance Programme (EAP). EAP's provide counselling, information and/or referral to appropriate counselling treatment and support services. Originally introduced in the USA to tackle alcohol related problems, the concept of workplace counselling has since assumed a significantly wider focus. Such services are confidential and usually provide a 24 hour telephone contact line. Employees are able to voluntarily access these services or in some cases are referred by their Occupational Health function. The implementation of comprehensive systems and procedures to facilitate and monitor the rehabilitation and return to work of employees who have suffered a stress related illness is another aspect of tertiary prevention.

Whilst an example of tertiary level prevention did not form part of the case studies, there is evidence to suggest that counselling is effective in improving the psychological well being of employees and has considerable cost benefits. Based on reports published in the US, figures typically show savings to investment rates of anywhere from 3:1 to 15:1 (Cooper & Cartwright, 1994). Such reports have not been without criticism; particularly as increasingly schemes are evaluated by the managed "care companies" responsible for their implementation and who frequently are under contract to deliver a pre-set dollar saving (Smith and Mahoney, 1989). However, evidence from established counselling programmes which have been rigorously evaluated, such as those introduced by Kennecott in the US and the UK Post Office, resulted in a reduction in absenteeism in one year of approximately 60%.. In the case of the UK experience (Cooper & Sadri, 1991) measures taken pre and post counselling showed significant improvements in the mental health and self esteem of the participating employees. However, there was no improvement in levels of employee job satisfaction and organizational commitment.

Like stress management programmes, counselling services can be particularly effective in helping employees deal with workplace stressors which cannot be changed and non-work related stress (i.e. bereavement, marital breakdown etc.); but which nevertheless tend to spillover into work life.

A Comparison of Interventions

While there is considerable activity at the secondary and tertiary level, primary or organizational level (stressor reduction) strategies are comparatively rare (Murphy, 1984).

This is particularly the case in the US and the UK. Organizations tend to prefer to introduce secondary and tertiary level interventions for several reasons:-

(i)   there is relatively more published data available on the cost benefit analysis of such programmes, particularly EAPs

(ii)   those traditionally responsible for initiating interventions i.e. the counsellors, physicians and clinicians responsible for health care, feel more comfortable with changing individuals than changing organizations (Ivancevich et al, 1990)

(iii)   it is considered easier and less disruptive to business to change the individual than to embark on any extensive and potentially expensive organizational development programme - the outcome of which may be uncertain (Cooper & Cartwright, 1994)

(iv)   they present a high profile means by which organizations can "be seen to be doing something about stress" and taking reasonable precautions to safeguard employee health.

Overall, evidence as to the success of interventions which focus at the individual level in isolation suggests that such interventions can make a difference in temporarily reducing experienced stress (Murphy, 1988). Generally, evidence as to the success of stress management training is confusing and imprecise (Elkin & Rosch, 1990) which possibly reflects the idiosyncratic nature of the form and content of this kind of training. Some recent studies, which have evaluated the outcome of stress management training have found a modest improvement in self reported symptoms and psychological indices of strain (Sallis et al, 1987; Reynolds, Taylor & Shapiro, 1993) but little or no change in job satisfaction, work stress or blood pressure. Participants on the Zeneca programme reported improvements in health, in the short term (i.e. 3 months post intervention). However, as was pointed out, it is important for the company to establish whether this situation continues in the longer term. Similarly, as discussed, counselling appears to be successful in treating and rehabilitating employees suffering from stress but as they are likely to re-enter the same work environment as job dissatisfied and no more committed to the organization than they were before, potential productivity gains may not be maximised. Firth-Cozens and Hardy (1992) have suggested that as symptom levels reduce as a result of clinical treatment for stress, job perceptions are likely to become more positive. However, such changes are likely to be short term if employees return to an unchanged work environment and its indigenous stressors. If, as has been discussed, such initiatives have little impact on improving job satisfaction, then it is more likely that the individual will adopt a way of coping with stress which may have positive individual outcomes, but has negative implications for the organization i.e. taking alternative employment.

The evidence concerning the impact of health promotion activities has reached similar conclusions. Research findings which have examined the impact of lifestyle changes and health habits provide support that any benefits may not necessarily be sustained. Lifestyle and health promotion activities appear to be effective in reducing anxiety, depression and psychosomatic distress but do not necessarily moderate the stressor-strain linkage. According to Ivancevich & Matteson (1988), after a few years 70% of individuals who attend such programmes revert to their previous lifestyle habits.

Furthermore, as most stress management programmes or lifestyle change initiatives are voluntary, this raises the issue as to the characteristics and health status of those participants who elect to participate. According to Sutherland & Cooper (1990) participants tend to be the "worried well" rather than the extremely distressed. Consequently, those employees who need most help and are coping badly are not reached by these initiatives. Also, sometimes access to such programmes is restricted to managers and relatively senior personnel within the organization. Given that smoking, alcohol abuse, obesity and coronary heart disease are more prevalent amongst the lower socio-economic groups, and that members of this group are likely to occupy positions within the organizational structure which they perceive afford them little or no opportunity to change or modify the stressors inherent in their working environment, the potential health of arguably the "most at risk" individuals are not addressed. Finally, the introduction of such programmes in isolation may serve to enhance employee perceptions of the organization as a caring employer; interested in their health and well being and so may contribute to create a "feel good" factor which is unlikely to be sustained if the work environment continues to remain stressful.

Secondary and tertiary level interventions have a useful role to play in stress prevention but as "stand alone" initiatives, they are not the complete answer unless attempts are also made to address the sources of stress itself (Cartwright, Cooper & Murphy, 1995). Cardiovascular fitness programmes may be successful in reducing the harmful effects of stress on the high-pressured executive but such programmes will not eliminate the stressor itself, which may be overpromtion or a poor relationship with his/her boss (Cooper & Cartwright, 1994). Identifying and recognising the problem and taking steps to tackle it, perhaps by negotiation i.e. a "front end" approach, might arguably arrest the whole process. If, as has been discussed, experienced stress is related to the individual's appraisal of an event or situation, an organization can reduce stress by altering the objective situation e.g. by job redesign.

A further limitation of secondary and tertiary level interventions is that they do not directly address the important issue of control. This is particularly critical in terms of the health of blue-collar workers. Research has shown (Karasek 1979) that jobs which place high demands on the individual but at the same time afford the individual little control or discretion (referred to as "decision latitude") are inherently stressful. Stress management training may heighten the awareness of workers to environmental stressors which may be affecting their health, but because as individuals they may lack the resource or positional power to change them, they may arguably even exacerbate the problem.

Again, there is not a great deal of research evidence which has evaluated the impact of primary level interventions on employee health and well being. However, what exists has been consistently positive, particularly in showing the long term beneficial effects (Quick 1979; Jackson 1983).

Treatment may, therefore, often be easier than prevention, but it may only be an effective short term strategy. In focusing at the outcome or "rear end" of the stress process (i.e. poor mental and physical health) and taking remedial action to redress that situation, the approach is essentially reactive and recuperative rather than proactive and preventative.

In summary, secondary and tertiary levels of intervention are likely to be insufficient in maintaining employee health without the complimentary approach of primary/stressor reduction initiatives. Secondary and tertiary level interventions may extend the physical and psychological resources of the individual, particularly in relation to stressors which cannot be changed but those resources are ultimately finite. Tertiary level interventions, such as the provision of counselling services are likely to be particularly effective in dealing with non work related stress. Evidence from the UK Post Office counselling programmes indicates that approximately a quarter of all problems presented concerned relationships outside of work. Organizations considering counselling schemes should recognise that counselling is a highly skilled business and requires extensive training. It is important to ensure that counsellors have recognised counselling skills training and have access to a suitable environment which allows them to conduct this activity in an ethical and confidential manner.

Chapter 5

Towards the creation of healthy organizations -
the wider implications

The previous sections (Chapters 3 and 4) emphasised the importance and potential cost benefits to the organization of introducing initiatives to reduce stress and promote employee health and well being in the workplace. As the case studies demonstrated, action to reduce stress at work is usually prompted by some organizational problem or crisis, for example, escalating rates of sickness absence or labour turnover. Consequently, actions tend to be driven by a desire to reduce or arrest costs (i.e. problem driven-negative motives) rather than the desire to maximise potential and improve competitive edge (i.e. gains driven-positive motives). The danger of this type of approach is that once sickness absence or labour turnover rates stabilise at an acceptable level, interventions may lose their impetus and be considered no longer necessary. It has to be recognised that stress is dynamic and in a rapidly changing environment, is unlikely to ever disappear completely, but needs to be regularly monitored and addressed. Organizations need to consider stress prevention not only as a means of cost reduction or containment but also as a means of maintaining and improving organizational health and increasing productivity. The costs of stress and the collective health and wealth of European organizations and their workers is of great importance to members of the European Union as a whole. Occupational stress is not just an organizational problem but a wider societal problem which is ultimately shared by all members of the EU, both directly and indirectly, through increased taxation and State health insurance contributions or diminished living standards as a result of loss of competitive edge. This final section is therefore concerned with the extent to which consolidated action and policies at Community level can address the problem of stress at work. It considers ways in which EU policymakers can encourage and provide information and incentives to responsible organizations to instigate and maintain stress intervention strategies.

1.   Risk Assessment

Legislative differences in Health and Safety matters within individual States would seem to influence practices, interpretation and employer attitudes.

The framework Directive on Health and Safety (89/391) embodies the concept of risk assessment which makes it mandatory for organizations within 15 member states to assess the health and safety risks to its workers. In terms of employer obligations, the important points of this Directive are:

-   the provision of protective, preventive and emergency services
-   comprehensive information in the area of health and safety, and
-   full consultation and participation rights to workers on matters affecting workplace health and safety

Stress represents an occupational risk to health. The assessment of psychosocial factors relating to health is substantially different from assessing physical hazard in the working environment which has been the traditional domain of the Labour and Factory Inspectorate and those responsible for Health and Safety within an organization. Concerns have been expressed (Wynne & Clarkin, 1992) as to the shortage of sufficiently trained personnel and the adequate provision of training in many countries to undertake the traditional tasks of occupational health and safety. Not surprisingly, there is likely to be an even greater skills and training deficiency in the area of psychosocial factors pertaining to health.

Therefore, in order to provide appropriate guidance and increase organizational awareness of these factors, investment is needed to provide comprehensive, professional and universal training for existing Labour and Factory Inspectors. Alternatively, there should be a move towards more interdisciplinary teams which include an expert trained in this field. This training should also be extended to managers and employee representatives within companies. By introducing regular risk assessments in this area, this would help organizations understand and monitor factors which may negatively affect employee health and psychological well being. Health and Safety authorities in individual member states have a major role to play in either conducting risk assessments themselves or providing appropriate advice and support to organizations to enable them to perform their own assessment.

2.   Economic Incentives

Typically, organizations respond to statutory legislation by implementing the minimum requirements to conform with the law. Rather than merely punishing "bad practice", the more effective way of encouraging "good practice" is to reward it. This could take the form of providing tax incentives for validated health and safety expenditure incurred by organizations as discussed in the recent European Foundation publication (Bailey, Jorgensen, Kruger & Litske, 1994).

Another option is to more directly link risk assessment and stress prevention strategies to insurance premiums. Currently, the cost of employee accidents and compensation for injuries and illness and negligence across Europe is met by a variety of insurance bodies in both the public and private sector. Insurance premiums may be levied as a flat rate or vary according to the claims experience of the industry sector or the individual organization. When premiums are linked to the claims experience or past accident history of the individual organization, employers become more aware of the true cost of their actions. If an employer is penalised by an increased premium as a result of a high accident rate, they are likely to take steps to address and improve the situation. However, there are drawbacks to such arrangements. For example, employers may put pressure on employees not to pursue claims or report accidents. Claims experience data based costs can give a distorted picture when there is a large payment made for a long term disability or fatality. Similarly, experience based solely on accident frequency rates may unfairly penalise an organization which has a lot of relatively inexpensive minor accidents compared to an organization with fewer, but which result in a more severe and costly outcome. These issues are particularly relevant to small and medium sized enterprises. Most importantly, experienced based insurance ratings focus on historical records and so do not take into account the efforts an organization may be making to reduce future risk. However, there would perhaps be some benefit in insurance providers pooling their collective experiences and statistics on an industry basis to help identify particular business sectors which might benefit from more specifically targeted Health & Safety initiatives.

A more effective and fairer way in which organizations could be rewarded for the efforts in creating more healthy working environments would be to link incentives to stress audits and the presence of stress intervention programmes. A rather similar scheme, the Work Injury Reduction Programme (WIRP) is currently being trialled in Alberta. Employers who have voluntarily opted to join the scheme are required to undergo an annual audit of their management systems. This audit focuses on six areas:

- corporate leadership
- operations
- human resources
- facilities and services
- administration
- health and safety information and promotion

The organization's performance is scored out of a possible 2,000 points to provide an index of progress. Employers are required to take action on the results of this audit and the report recommendations in order to qualify for financial incentives. The potential exists for large companies to receive incentives as high as $2 million (approximately ECU 1.5 million).

3.   Specific Assistance for Small and Medium Sized Enterprises

The case study examples, in reflecting current practice, were drawn from large organizations; although the initial projects concerned relatively small production units within these large concerns. The low participation of SMEs in stress prevention and health promotion activities is a source of concern, since SMEs form a major proportion of EU businesses; with some 40% of companies employing less than 10 people and around 60% with less than 50 (Bailey, Jorgensen, Kruger & Litske, 1994). This may be due to lack of resources; lack of skilled personnel or lack of access to information. Time and financial costs are more problematic for smaller companies. The pricing structure of Employee Assistance Programmes means that these kinds of services are generally not available on an individual basis to SMEs. Only 44% of EU workers are covered by in plant or have access to group Occupational Health Services (Wayne & Clarkin, 1992). Access to stress management training provided by external agencies is significantly more limited and difficult for SMEs. Certainly, the provision of more Government/community funded training opportunities and easier and more open access to information and courses specifically targeted at SMEs would help in this respect.

Another possible way in which SMEs could access professional help and expertise would be for companies to combine to share the costs of preventative services, along the lines of group practice models operating in some EU member states, e.g. The Netherlands.   In the Netherlands, all employees have access to a panel of professionals who will provide them with Occupational Health and Health and Safety Services. These services are funded by levies paid by the organization based on the size of their workforce. In Sweden prior to 1995, all organizations paid a levy into a central fund, the Working Life Fund, which provided employers with access to professional help and expertise on work related health issues which they could call upon for advice on organizational problems. In addition to providing information and guidance, the Working Life Fund undertook specific projects at corporate level. The combination of these two kinds of services to provide assistance to both employees and employers would be greatly beneficial to SMEs.

4.   More Information and Research

The level of research activity in the area of occupational stress and stress prevention varies considerably from country to country, as does the level of organizational activity. Much more research is needed, particularly studies which evaluate the long term effectiveness of stress intervention strategies.   There is also much to be learnt from the dissemination of more practical case studies of organizational practice and experience in stress prevention. Stronger industrial links between the business community and academic institutions can promote this type of activity, particularly as the Dutch case study illustrates, when there is some joint investment.

The conventional sources of research funding provided through Government research grants awarded to academic institutions are increasingly limited. This suggests that alternative sources of funding may be needed to ensure that the research activity keeps pace with the demand for knowledge.

References

Chapter 1

Baker, D.B. (1985). "The Study of Stress at Work" Annual Review of Public Health, 6 367-381.

Beehr, T.A. (1995). Psychological Stress in the Workplace. London : Routledge.

Cartwright, S. (1995 in press). "Human resource policy today: The challenges of a changing business environment" Business Studies.

Cartwright, S. & Cooper, C.L. (1994). No Hassle: Taking the Stress out of Work. London: Century Business.

Commission of the European Communities (1992). European Year of Safety, Hygiene and Health Protection at Work.

Cooper, C.L. (1995). Handbook of Stress, Medicine and Health. Florida: CRC Press.

Cooper, C.L. & Cartwright, S. (1994). "Healthy mind, healthy organization: A proactive approach to stress management" Human Relations, 47(4), 455-471.

Cooper, C.L. & Payne, R. (1988). Causes, Coping and Consequences of Stress at Work. Chichester: John Wiley & Sons.

Cooper, C.L. & Williams, S. (1994). (eds) Creating Healthy Work Organizations. Chichester: John Wiley & Sons.

Cox, T. (1978). Stress. London : Macmillan.

Cummings, T., & Cooper, C.L. (1979). "A Cybernetic Framework for the Study of Occupational Stress". Human Relations, 32, 395-419.

Davidson, M.J. & Coopers, C.L. (1993). (eds). Women in Business and Management. London: Paul Chapman Publishers.

de Gier, E., Kompier, M., Draaisma, D and Smulders, P. (1994). The legislation policy and practice concerning the prevention of stress at work in the Netherlands, United Kingdom, Germany and France in European Foundation for the Improvement of Living and Working Conditions. European Conference on Stress at Work - A call for action : Proceedings. Luxembourg : Official Publication of the European Communities.

DeFrank, R.S. & Cooper, C.L. (1987). "Worksite stress management interventions: Their effectiveness and conceptualisation" Journal of Managerial Psychology, 2, 4-10.

Elkin, A.J. & Rosch, P.J. (1990). "Promoting mental health at the workplace: The prevention side of stress management". Occupational Medicine: State of the Art Review, 5(4), 739-754.

European Foundation for the Improvement of Living and Working Conditions (1993). European Conference on Stress at Work - A Call for Action : Proceedings. Brusssels: 9-10 November. Luxembourg: Office for Official Publications of the European Communities.

European Foundation for the Improvement of Living and Working Conditions (1992). First European Survey on the Work Environment 1991-1992. Luxembourg: Office for Official Publications of the European Communities.

Frese, M. (1985). "Stress at work and psychosomatic complaints: A causal interpretation". Journal of Applied Psychology, 70, 314-328.

Harris, L. & Associates (1985). Poll conducted for the Metropolitan Life Foundation.

Ivancevich, J.M. & Matteson, M.T. (1980). Stress and Work: A Managerial Perspective. Glenview Illinois : Scott Foresman.

Johnson, J.V. & Johansson, G. (eds). (1991). The Psychosocial Work Environment: Work Organization, Democratization and Health. Amityville, New York: Bayhood Publishing Company.

Karasek, R. & Theorell, T. (1990). Healthy Work: Stress, Productivity and the Reconstruction of Working Life. New York: John Wiley & Sons.

Lazarus, R.S. (1976). Patterns of Adjustment. New York : McGraw-Hill.

Lunde-Jensen, P. (1994). "The costs of occupational accidents and work-related sickness in the Nordic countries". Janus, No. 18(4). 25-26.

Newman, J.E. & Beehr, T.A. (1979). "Personal and organizational strategies for handling job stress: a review of research and opinion". Personnel Psychology, 32, 1-43.

McLean, A.A. (1980). Workstress. Reading, MA: Addison Wesley.

Palmer, S. (1989). "Occupational Stress" Health & Safety Practitioner, August 1989. 16-18.

Selye, H. (1946). "The General Adaptation Syndrome and the Disease of Adaptation". Journal of Clinical Endocrinology, 6, 117.

Sigman, A. (1992). "The state of corporate health care". Personnel Management, February. 47-61.

Wynne, R. & Clarkin, N. (1992). Under construction: Building for health in the EC workplace. Dublin: European Foundation for the Improvement of Living and Working

Chapter 2

Case Study II

CBI-PERCOM Survey (1994). Sickness Absence. London: CBI-PERCOM.

Dijk, F. van, Dormolen, M. van. Kompier, M., and T. Myman (1990). Herwaardering model belasting-belastbaarheid. T. Soc. Gezondheidszorg, 3-10.

Draaisma, D., Grundemann, R.W.M., and H. Hoolboom (1991). Werk en gezondheid van uitvoerders in longitudinaal perspectief I. T. Soc. Gezondheidszorg, 480-488.

Grundemann, R.W.M., Draaisma, D., and H. Hoolboom (1992). Werk en gezondheid can uitvoerders inlongitudinaal perspectief II. T. Soc. Gezondheidszorg, 103-110.

Israel, B.A., Schurman, S.J., and J.S. House (1989). Action research on occupational stress: involving workers as researchers. Int. J. of Health Services, 135-155.

Murphy, L R. (1988). Workplace Interventions for Stress Reduction and Prevention. In. C.L. Cooper and R. Payne, Causes, Coping and Consequences of Stress at Work. Chichester: John Wiley & Sons, 301-339.

Nijhuis, F.J.N. (1994). Health & Safety: Integrated health promotion programmes aimed at changing work conditions and work behaviour. In. C. Johansen, Proceedings of the Conference Work and Health, Copenhagen.

Offermans, X., Meijers, J.M., Nijhuis, F., Rijssen-Moll, M. van, and Tj. de Boorder (1988). Bedrijfsgezondheidszorg voor het vernoerswezen in Nederland. Gezondheidsrisico's structuur en inhound. The Hague, Ministry of Social Affairs, S-38.

Prins, R. (1990). Sickness absence in Belgium, Germany (FR) and the Netherlands, a comparative study. Maastricht: Rijksuniversiteit Limburg.

Sutherland, V.J. and Davidson, M.J. (1993). Using a stress audit: the construction site manager experience in the UK. Work & Stress, 273-286.

Case Study III

Cooper, C.L. & Marshall, J. (1980). White Collar and Professional Stress. Chichester & New York: John Wiley & Sons.

Friedman, M., Thoresen, C.E., Gill, J.J., Ulmer, D., Powell, L.H., Price, V.A., Brown, B., Thompson, L., Rabin, D.D., Breall, W.S., Bourg, E., Levy, R. and Dixon, T. (1986). Alternation of type A behaviour and its effect on cardiac recurrences in post-myocardial infarction patients: Summary of result of the recurrent coronary prevention project. <u>American Heart Journal</u>, <u>12(4)</u>, 653-665.

Ornish, D., Brown, S.E., Scherwitz, L.W., Billings, J.H., Armstrong, W.T., Ports, T.A., McLanahan, S.M., Kirkeeide, R.L., Brand, R.J. and Lance Gould, K. (1990). Can lifestyle changes reverse coronary heart disease? The Lifestyle Heart Trial. <u>Lancet</u>, <u>336</u>, 129-133.

Patel, C. and Marmot, M. (1988). Can general practitioners use training in relaxation and management of stress to reduce mild hypertension? <u>British Medical Journal</u>, <u>296</u>, 21-24.

Chapter 3

Cooper, C.L. & Cartwright, S. (1994). "Healthy Mind, Healthy Organization - A proactive approach to Occupational Stress". <u>Human Relations</u>, <u>47(4)</u>, 455-471.

Levi, L. & Lunde-Jensen, P. (1996 in press). Socio-economic Costs of Work Stress in two EU Member States : A model for assessment of the costs of stress at the national level". Dublin: European Foundation for the Improvement of Living and Working Conditions.

O'Donnell, M.P. (1984). <u>The Corporate Perspective</u> in O'Donnell, M.P. and Ainsworth, T. (eds). <u>Health Promotion in the Workplace</u>. New York: John Wiley & Sons. p.10-37

Nilson, N. (1995). "Power to the People". <u>Scanorama</u>. July/August, 91-92.

Chapter 4

Cartwright, S., Cooper, C.L. & Murphy, L.R. (1995 in press). "Diagnosing a healthy organization: A proactive approach to stress in the workplace" in Keita, G.P. and Sauter, S. (eds). <u>Job Stress Intervention: Current Practice and Future Directions</u>. APA/NIOSH, Washington, DC.

Cooper, C.L. & Cartwright, S. (1994). "Healthy Mind, Healthy Organization - A proactive approach to Occupational Stress". <u>Human Relations</u>, <u>47(4)</u>, 455-471.

Cooper, C.L. & Sadri, G. (1991). "The impact of stress counselling at work" in Perrewe, P.L. (ed). Handbook of Job Stress (Special Issue). <u>Journal of Social Behaviour and Personality</u>, <u>6(7)</u>, 411-423.

Cox, T. (1978). <u>Stress</u>. London: MacMillan.

Edwards, J.R. & Cooper, C.L. (1990). The person-environment fit approach to stress: Recurring problems and some suggested solutions. <u>Journal of Organizational Behaviour</u>, <u>11</u>, 293-307.

Elkin, A.J. & Rosch, P.J. (1990). "Promoting mental health at the workplace: the prevention side of stress management". <u>Occupational Medicine: State of the Art Review</u>, <u>5(4)</u>, 739-754.

Firth-Cozens, J. & Hardy, C.E. (1992). "Occupational stress, clinical treatment, change in job perception". Journal of Occupational and Organizational Psychology, 65, 81-88.

Jackson, S.E. (1983). "Participation in decision making as a strategy for reducing job related strain". Journal of Applied Psychology, 68, 3-19.

Ivancevich, J. M., Matteson, M.T., Freedman, S.M. & Phillips, J.S. (1990). Worksite stress management interventions. American Psychologist, 45, 252-261

Ivancevich, J.M. & Matteson, M.T. (1988). "Promoting the individual's health and well being" in Cooper, C.L. and Payne, R. (eds) Causes, Coping and Consequences of Stress at Work. Chichester & New York: John Wiley & Sons.

Karasek, R.A. (1979). "Job demands, decision latitude and mental strain: Implications for job design". Administrative Science Quarterly, 24, 285-307.

Kompier, M., De Gier, E., Smulders, P. & Draaisma, D. (1994). Regulations, policies and practices concerning work stress in five European countries. Work and Stress, 8, (4), 296-318.

Murphy, L.R. (1984). "Occupational stress management: A review and appraisal". Journal of Occupational Psychology, 57, 1-15.

Murphy, L.R. (1988). "Workplace interventions for stress reduction and prevention" in Cooper, C.L. and Payne, R. (eds). Causes, Coping and Consequences of Stress at Work. Chichester & New York: John Wiley & Sons.

Quick, J.C. (1979). "Dyadic goal setting and role stress in field study". Academy of Management Journal, 22, 241-252.

Reynolds, S., Taylor, E. and Shapiro, D.A. (1993). "Session impact in stress management training". Journal of Occupational and Organizational Psychology, 66, 99-113.

Sallis, J.F., Trevorrow, T.R., Johnson, C.C., Howell, M.F. & Kaplan, R.M. (1984). "Worksite stress management: A comparison of programmes". Psychology and Health, 1, 237-255.

Sauter, S., Murphy, L.R. & Hurrell, J.J. Jnr. (1990). "A national strategy for the prevention of work related psychological disorders". American Psychologist, 45, 1146-1158.

Smith, D. & Mahoney, J. (1989). "McDonnell Douglas Corporation's EAP produces hard data". The Almacan, August, 18-26.

Sutherland, V.J. & Cooper, C.L. (1990). Understanding Stress. London: Chapman & Hall.

Chapter 5

European Foundation for the Improvement of Living and Working Conditions (1994). Economic incentives to improve the working environment. Authors: S. Bailey., K. Jorgensen., W. Kruger and H. Litske. Luxembourg: Official Publication of the European Communities.

European Foundation for the Improvement of Living and Working Conditions (1994). Stress at Work: Causes, Effects and Prevention: A guide for small and medium sized enterprises. Authors: M. Kompier and L. Levi. Luxembourg: Official Publication of the European Communities.

European Foundation for the Improvement of Living and Working Conditions (1992). Under construction: Building for health in the EC workplace. Authors: R. Wynne and N. Clarkin. Luxembourg: Official Publication of the European Communities.

Useful Names and Addresses

National Addresses

Österreichisches Bundesinstitut
für Gesundheitswesen
Stubenring 6
A-1010 Vienna
AUSTRIA

ANPAT/NWA
Rue Gachard 88, bte. 4
B-1050 Brussels
BELGIUM

Arbejdstilsynet
Landskronagade 33-35
DK-2100 Copenhagen O
DENMARK

Finnish Institute of Occupational Health
Topeliuksenkatu 41 a A
00250 Helsinki
FINLAND

Agence Nationale pour l'Amélioration
des Condition de Travail (ANACT)
7 Boulevard Romain Rolland
92128 Montrouge
FRANCE

Bundesanstalt fûr Arbeitsschutz
Friedrich-Henkel-Weg 1-25
D-44149 Dortmund (Dorstfeld)
GERMANY

Bundesanstalt fûr Arbeitsmedizin
Nôldnerstrasse 40-42
D-10317 Berlin
GERMANY

Greek Institute for Health & Safety at Work (ELINYAE)
Patison 89
GR-104 34 Athens
GREECE

Health and Safety Authority
Hogan Place
Dublin 2
IRELAND

Offices des Assurances Sociales
125 route d'Esch
L-2976 Luxembourg
LUXEMBOURG

Instituto de Desenvovimento e Inspecção das
Condiçôes de Trabalho do
Ministério do Emprego e da
Segurança Social
Praça de Londres 2-10
1000 Lisboa
PORTUGAL

Nederlands Institut voor
Arbeidsomstandigheden (NIA)
Postbus 75665
1070 AR Amsterdam
NETHERLANDS

TNO Institute of Preventive Health Care
Postbus 124
2300 AC Leiden
NETHERLANDS

Instituto National de Seguridad e
Higiene en el Trabajo
Torrelaguna 73
28027 Madrid
SPAIN

Stress Research Section
Karolinska Instituet
PO Box 220
S-171 77 Stockholm
SWEDEN

Arbetslivinstitutet
S-17184 Solna
SWEDEN

Health & Safety Executive
Broad Lane
Sheffield S3 7HQ
UNITED KINGDOM

European Addresses

European Trade Union Confederation (ETUC)
Boulevard Emile Jacqmain 155
B-1210 Brussels
BELGIUM

Union des Confédéations de l'Industrie et
des Employeurs d'Europe (UNICE)
rue Joseph II, 40
B-1040 Brussels
BELGIUM

The European Foundation for
the Improvement of Living and Working Conditions
Lounglinstown House
Shankill
Co. Dublin
IRELAND

Euroepan Commission
DGV/F/5, Luxembourg
Bâtiment Jean Monnet
L-2920 Luxembourg
LUXEMBOURG

Health & Safety Agency
Bilbao
SPAIN
(Address still not available)

International Labour Office (ILO)
4 rue des Morrillons
CH-1211 Genève 22
SWITZERLAND

European Foundation for the Improvement of Living and Working Conditions

Stress Prevention in the Workplace:
Assessing the Costs and Benefits to Organisations

Luxembourg: Office for Official Publications of the European Communities, 1996

1996 — 120 pp. – 16 x 23.4 cm

ISBN 92-827-6503-2

Price (excluding VAT) in Luxembourg: ECU 11.50